DARYL HINE
SELECTED
POEMS

with best wishes

Hopkins

Daryl Hine

ATHENEUM
New York
1981

BOOKS BY DARYL HINE

POETRY
Daylight Saving 1978
Resident Alien 1975
In and Out 1975
Minutes 1968
The Wooden Horse 1965
The Devil's Picture Book 1961
The Carnal and the Crane 1957
Five Poems 1954

FICTION
The Prince of Darkness and Co. 1961

TRAVEL
Polish Subtitles 1962

TRANSLATION
The Homeric Hymns *and* The Battle of the Frogs
and the Mice 1972

Poems from the following previously published books are
included in the present volume of *Selected Poems:*

FIVE POEMS, 1955
THE CARNAL AND THE CRANE, copyright 1957 by Daryl Hine
THE DEVIL'S PICTURE BOOK, copyright © 1960 by Daryl Hine
THE WOODEN HORSE, copyright © 1960, 1962, 1963, 1964, 1965 by Daryl Hine
MINUTES, copyright © 1965, 1966, 1967, 1968 by Daryl Hine
RESIDENT ALIEN, copyright © 1975 by Daryl Hine
DAYLIGHT SAVING, copyright © 1978 by Daryl Hine

Contents

Contents

4

From DAYLIGHT SAVING

For Samuel Todes

LINES ON A PLATONIC FRIENDSHIP

Virtue was the sunset creeping in the grass
Or fireworks supplied with paradise;
But surely the day has come and gone—
The regal chestnuts burning in the ice—
When you could hold my face in the burning-glass
And flash a hole to China through my flesh.

You will search the skies to bring me down
Because I shall escape to other suns
Reflected in the geographic calm.
It seems to me your love was like a gun
That could break into the blind, myself,
With a racket like a hunter falling down,
Showing us how to capture through the trees
Palaces to house the widowed fox
And Captain Courage dead among the phlox.

Whenever I wished we used to talk of vice
Holding his chessmen balanced in the glass
Or suddenly illuminating flesh;
While a bee for beauty boomed behind the grove
Exploding comments on the world of love
Above a hill that shone like bone;
Not as you would think, white and smooth,
But a mangled affair of feathers guts and blood
In the wide and waveless waters of the wood.

The sun will set among these sacred pits
Filled with gillyflowers and cats
Rephrasing silence till the silence fits.
Sleepers will wake upon the precipice,
Their beardless faces sunburnt by the glass;
Guides or strangers in my place.
And you, whom virtue beautifies no more,
Where the print ends like a wave upon the page
Indicate a comment in the margin:
'Love's a shadow like a current in the garden.'

A LA RECHERCHE

Now over all the pictures in the house,
The small hand-mirror and the tall pier-glass
Wherein androgyne Albertine appears
(A winter landscape harbouring few grouse),
There courses Bluebeard with his magic axe,
A Grecian guidebook and a bag of tricks.
On either side the ruined road
Reflections from his hothouse spread,
The empty fields, still effigies of light,
Towering, translucent, out of sight.

You will not find it on the tourist maps,
But on that ideal one, perhaps,
With which one covers islands in the walls,
Where for many miles the water falls
Or seems to fall, reverting to the South
Past transparent monuments to youth.
The final word across in our acrostic:
The dead may know; the living are agnostic.

Several times before you reach the place
You have to ask directions, and each time
Strangers assume a different kind of grace;
Now naked, now disfigured by some crime,
Beneath the paper hat the paper face
Is delivered of its tesselated line:
'What if, amid such very varied scenes,
Your passenger grew tired of magazines,
And leans against your shoulder for a nap?
The marvellous book falls open on your lap
At certain hours wasted in a field
While a single airplane faltered overhead.

'The poet is always settled in the midst of winter.
At most, the sun is his only fire,
Whose indifferent candle
Cannot occlude the soul's window,
While he, manipulating mirrors
Flatters and frightens an audience of terrors.
Outside of this the absent fields are dead.
The hothouse alone supports the idle weed.'

Flowers attain serenity after death—
From this illusion glasses gain their depth.
The counties of desire are divorced,
And frail conveyors of conception, lost,
Like passions represented in a fable.
But what we want to see's a constable;
Beyond the hothouse wall, upon the lawn,
The summerhouse conceals a wounded man:
Beyond that, there's an artificial lake.
The guidebook drones and it is growing dark.

How pleasant it is here upon the water!
Where every wavelet, bowing, is a waiter
In whose unfathomed gaze we see ourselves
Part desire, part reflection, and part flesh.
The victim we had guessed at vaguely swings
From lighted rafters upon leaded wings.
The lake's a mirage! the garden's a disgrace!
And all the fish we thought we'd caught must face
Angelic parodies of time and place.

THE LESSON OF ANATOMY

For Jay Macpherson

This innocent device between fire and water
That the curious child chilled and discomposed,
Whose vocal effort in the tinder forest
Was intimacy mistaken, innocence forsaken,
And the wintry road to pleasure finally closed,
Moved to tears, I shall describe to you;
So listen hard and turn the nodding head to
                                        knowing's intimacy now.
Pretend the body lies upon the water,
And out of the mouth the mind,
Whose torment limns
Illusions of all sweet things in time,
Examines its grave and igneous lineaments.

'My head, my torso, and my hands and feet
Are drawn in white, like curiosities
Or continents left whiter by the flood.
Look closely at the movement of my blood:
In a lull, the body's sudden trough
Shows you the quiet Laplands of my breath,
Where my organs, when they do not freeze,
Sing, occasionally handsome, in the trees.'

Whether these lines will tremble in the fire
And all the lively passions there contract:
The mouth taste always the January apple,
The eyes be sweetened by perpetual desire,
Like captains and kings for nothing blackened,
And the crowned head go innocent into battle,
Like all the other senses, cerebral,
I cannot answer. You alone can tell.

That simple physicality is done
And dies instead of robins flying South
Of too great an intimacy with the sun,
You're bound to think so to believe the
                                    orgiasts undone.
Recall the elaborate folly of their youth,
And that the crowned cadaver on the table,
Like winter stories of the cold-hearted furies,
Fool fire extinguished, runs away like water.
So diagram it now, and memorize its form while you
                                    are able.

FABULARY SATIRE IV

The fox and crow, their dirty business finished,
Each in the aqueous landscape played his part,
Moved by the sun that shone on honour tarnished
And motivated by a love of art.
And through the leaves of trees their argument
Seemed to extend the empire of the heart;
Each claimed to be the other's monument,
And like the jack each called the queen a tart.

Fox

Was it you or some indifferent stranger
Put by my bed the bottle labelled Danger?

Crow

It was I. There never was a stranger
Could understand your hunger.
But who was it hid the bomb inside the bower
And wrote Fuck You across the bathroom mirror?

Fox

It was I, to crystallize your fever
With love's check and love's thermometer.

The crow considered talk ephemeral
And thought outmoded once the reed was broken.
The fox thought of the progress of the soul
And if indigestion meant the crow had spoken.
The cause of satire dying in his mind,
He turned the dialogue to those forsaken,
Whether they, like vox and trumpet in the wind,
Might someday talk of continence unshaken.

Crow

It is impossible to live in a world with animals
Who need a sunlit and immoral place,
To whom our problems are chimerical,
And who make right and wrong wait on table.

Fox

To animals the world is animal—
The only one that suffered was the cheese,
Who was after all the subject of the fall,
But who is seldom mentioned in the fable.

A BEWILDERMENT AT THE ENTRANCE
OF THE FAT BOY INTO EDEN

'L'art ne me connaît pas; je ne connais pas l'art.'
—CORBIÈRE

i

Not knowing where he was or how he got there,
Led by the gentle sessions of his demons,
Now in the right and now in the left ear,
The fat boy trod ungarlanded in Eden.
Perhaps he knew of nowhere else to go.
Affairs of the heart, concerns of money, too,
Deprived him of all choosing of his route.
Dreaming of disaster, he set foot
At midnight in the earthly paradise.
The ice around him shattered like a shot,
The gates swung open, and an angel stood,
(His bright sword averted and put up),
To watch the fat boy lollop from the wood
He couldn't see because he was asleep.

ii

Within his head a rank and silent fortune
Gestured slowly. On the silver screen
Papier-mâché herds of buffalo
Pursued a cowboy over endless prairie,
While down his cheeks the glittering orbs of sorrow
Rolled their separate tracks to final ruin.
What password did his virtues and his powers
Whisper, that he awoke within the gates,
Preserved against his enemies the hours,
While we who, like the vultures near the towers,
Live at the expense of those who die of boredom,
Enchained by the strait enchantment of their longing,
Must pitch our camp beneath the walls of Sodom,
Detained within the sweet preserves of time?

iii

Always through the badlands of the heart
The invisible posse kept a secret watch.
Across the desert of the intellect,
Murmured his persuaders, Forward march!
Lest mirage of thought too intricate distract
The sight, or sound amuse the hearing
Whose ignorance alone they might instruct,
They guarded their somnambulist, and laid
His ears in stillness and his eyes in shade,
And on his tongue the sesame of love:
A little word so common in the world.
All doors were opened to him. What he meant:
The sentiment, the purpose, or the act,
He couldn't say and never understood.

iv

A little word. Unconsciousness is all.
But all our wisdom is unwillingness.
We cannot blink the lightning of the wit,
Or sink the ego's fragile paper boat.
We think too much. Our selves are ponderous.
Only the fat boy bounces like a ball
The law set rolling into the lawless park:
Contemptible, unintroduced to art.
His demon is our muse, when, after dark,
Each must choose a mask and play a part:
I'll be Hamlet or Polonius,
Or the deuce, whichever face will fit.
And I, Ophelia, who, in her distress,
Interbound the bitter with the sweet.

THE WOUND

Tomorrow will the wound be quickly healed,
Or mutual. You will then be well,
Or we united by a common ill,
Division from the womb be reconciled.
But see how slow it bleeds!
Beside the heaving impasse of the boar,
Whose tusks he once preferred to Eros' reeds,
Under Venus' care Adonis bleeds
Of the wound he suffered at the kill.
See how she bends above him still
And takes what he would not bestow before!

In a while the bleeding slowly stops:
For the time being you are cured and whole.
For that duration who will comfort me?
We profit from each other's injury,
We change with wounding, wounded are transformed.
The oriole, they say, sings best when blind;
For ostentation is the peacock penned,
And everyone knows about the chrysalis,
That time's limp is his aggrandisement.

The hurt you entertained, you say,
Was like the mark an arrow leaves in exit:
Round and not too large, contagion's portal.
The target that the arrow makes is joy.
My own mutilation as a fiction
I sustained, I thought alone, for weeks,
Until by habit turned in your direction,
I felt the shared blood running down your cheeks.

UNDER THE HILL

The gates fly open with a pretty sound,
Nor offer opposition to the knight.
A sensual world, remote, extinct, is found.

In walls that like luxurious thorns surround
The exquisite lewdness of the sybarite,
The gates fly open with a pretty sound.

Where venery goes hunting like a hound,
And all the many mouths of pleasure bite,
A sensual world, remote, extinct, is found.

The passionate pilgrim strayed beneath the ground
Meets only death, until, to his delight,
The gates fly open with a pretty sound.

In Venus' clutches, under Venus' mound,
He whiles away the long venereal night.
A sensual world, remote, extinct, is found.

The single function on which Venus frowned
Was birth; and, maybe, life has proved her right.
The gates fly open with a pretty sound.
A sensual world, remote, extinct, is found.

THE DOUBLE-GOER

All that I do is clumsy and ill timed.
You move quickly, when it must be done,
To spare yourself or save your victim pain.
And then like the light of the sun you move away
While I come face to face with complex crime
Far from the moving of the mellifluous sea.
All that I do is clumsy and ill timed.
When you perform, my errors pantomimed
    Will give an example to the sun
    Of flight, and to shadows how to run.
You will in turn discover in my rhyme
Justifications for your simple crime.

Manifold are the disguises of our love.
We change, our transformations turn about,
Our shadowy forms become the doubles for
Affection or hatred. Yet a kind of growth
Is visible, and may be termed the heart,
Confused by the ambiguities of our art.
Manifold are the disguises of our love.
Contradiction of terms is all we have.
    To please the self and then the soul
    Is difficult and terrible;
Impossible to own a single heart
Lost in the double-dealing of our art.

Two-edged is the double-goer's tongue,
Malice and honey, and the prizes in
His logomachy, what lie near the heart:
Money, honour and success in love.
Harmonious ambiguities in a swarm
Burrow at the fulcrum of his speech.
Two-edged is the double-goer's tongue.

One side says, Right, the other side says, Wrong;
   One, Love is red, the other, Black;
   One, Go on, and one, Turn back.
One hopes for heaven, one for earth, and each
To strike a concord through cross-purposed
      speech.

So split and halved and twain is every part,
So like two persons severed by a glass
Which darkens the discerning whose is whose
And gives two arms for love and two for hate,
That they cannot discover what they're at
And sometimes think of killing and embrace.
So split and halved and twain is every part,
Double the loins, the fingers, and the heart,
   Confused in object and in aim,
   That they cannot their pleasure name,
But like two doubles in a darkened place
Make one obscure assault and one embrace.

For they were to duality born and bred.
From their childhood the powers of evil were
No less their familiar than the mirror,
Source of a comfortable terror now and then,
And romantic: What good is a fiend unless
I can think and he, my double, act?
Thus we were to duality born and bred.
If these two eyes could turn in the one head,
   Bright orbs by a brighter sphere enclosed,
   Mutually blind and self-opposed,
The right supplying what the left one lacked,
Then I can think, and you, my body, act.

In singleness there is no heart or soul
And solitude is scarcely possible.
The one-sailed ship, tossed on a divided sea
As lightly as cork is tossed, as blindly as
The partners toss on their oceanic bed
And rise and fall, is wrecked and lost away.
In singleness there is no heart or soul;
Thus he sees wrong who sees in halves a whole,
    Who searches heaven but for one,
    And not a double of the sun,
Forgets that, being light as cork, the day
Can rise or fall, is wrecked and lost away.

All that I do is careless and sublime.
You walk head-downwards, now your opened
        eyes
Take comfort from the beauty of the site.
What if the vision vary in detail?
What are we but sleepers in a cave,
Our dreams the shades of universal doubt?
All that I do is careless and sublime,
You bore with patience to the heart of time;
    Though your resource of art is small
    And my device yields none at all,
Still this two-handed engine will find out
In us the shape and shadow of our doubt.

THE DESTRUCTION OF SODOM

One would never suspect there were so many vices.
It is, I think, a tribute to the imagination
Of those who in these eminently destructible cities
Have made an exact science of perversion
That they, like us, limited by their bodies,
Could put those bodies to such various uses.

Before now men have been punished for their uses
Contrary to nature, though some, indulging phantom vices
Secretly in the brothels of the imagination,
Have escaped so far a condemnation like these cities'
Which were rebuked for innocent perversion
Through the spirit's envy of too simple bodies.

Do not suppose that I intend to praise their bodies,
Though I admit that bodies have their uses,
Nor is my purpose to defend their vices.
Simply as a pervert of the imagination
I pronounce the funeral oration of two cities
Famous for acts of unimaginable perversion.

All love deserves the epitaph 'Perversion',
Being unnaturally concerned, like physics, with foreign
    bodies,
Inseparable from their uses and abuses.
To those who care for nothing but their vices
Love is the faculty of the imagination.
Fantasy, I say, debauches cities.

Discreetly, Lord, show mercy to these cities,
Not for the sake of their, but your, perversion
That contradicts its own created bodies.
These are precisely the instruments grace uses,
Alchemically reforming virtues of their vices,
To raise a heaven from the imagination.

O, where is that heaven of the imagination,
The first and least accessible of cities,
If not in the impossible kingdom of perversion?
Its angels have no sexes and no bodies,
Its speech, no words, its instruments, no uses.
None enter there but those who know their vices.

Number your vices in imagination:
Would they teach whole cities of perversion?
Forgive us our bodies, forgive our bodies' uses.

A TOUR IN THE FOREST

Here the bees live and the bears,
Industry and clumsiness
Met in the secret, chambered wood
To gauge each other's properties.
Here the powers of darkness brood
Among the cedars and the firs.

Desire, an unreflecting dusk
In which the sunlight errs and glances,
Performs love's labours, light denied,
Helped by the twilight of the senses.
Noonday alters to a shade.
Landscape turns into a mask.

Other than the animals,
Indifferent how remote they live
Imprisoned in the honeycomb,
The only creatures to survive
The forest loneliness and gloom
Are certain branded criminals,

Condemned, and, as they think, escaped.
But even here they are pursued,
Though less by judgments than by crimes:
The forest cut down and destroyed,
The old, obscure, anarchic dreams,
The victims slaughtered as they slept.

Why did we ever come here? Why
Has our conviction led us North
Into perpetual evening,
Where boredom paces back and forth
Like a lion ravening
Seeking whom he may destroy?

The eyes of travellers are glazed
By intolerance of everything they see:
Here, surely, no one good remains?
Animals not you and I
Lie beneath the evergreens,
Asleep, and fail to be surprised.

OSIRIS DISMEMBERED

If you in these divided limbs residing,
Your eye distending carefully to see
Obelisks and pyramids receding,
Colossi touched to music by the day,
Tuneful stone, light's mnemonic tiding,
Were really you and none of your five senses,
So you could swear, whatever I shall do
It may be yours but not yourself that winces
In involuntary agony, opposing to
Violence inviolable defences;
By the sweetness of your death preserved,
As honeybees in amber seem to live,
Immutable however you are carved,
Though riddled, beautiful as honeycomb or sieve,
You would be one who drew a death deserved.

The ultimate barque to bear you down the river
Through fruitful deserts, past the unasking sphinx,
Away from your dismemberer forever,
Approaches shore. The eye upon it winks,
Though painted; though becalmed, the wide sails quiver.
The time has come, the water in a witty
Parody of bees' funereal note
Murmurs as it wears against the jetty.
Ironic woe supports the sable boat.
The waves say, The queen has gone from the insect city.
Mourning hangs from the mast like leaves in November.
Water is glad that the king of the harvest is dead
And the god of the sun extinguished like an ember,
From the mouth in a vapour the sensible principle sped,
Rigour like ice in—on—each separate member.

But part and part by the waves of affection rolled,
Wakened by moving though they move apart—
Motion is heat—but to advances cold
As flight or fright or mercenary heart
Abandoning a pose it cannot hold
Is pain in my undying members hiding:
The eye must wink because it hates to see
A creature of its own division bleeding,
The mouth be chaste because it hurts to say
The formula and promise of dividing.
Drop by drop your veins my hands bedizen
Till I seem like the hive's destroyer, stung
In destructive act and blind with the insects' poison.
Can you tell me, with your torn-out tongue,
Is it light you look for under the horizon?

PSYCHE

Precious little is kept in Psyche's whatnot:
Baubles, curious postcards, clues and tangles
Of string—everything you might look for in the
Bulging pockets of thoughtless schoolboys, all but
Hands. There ought to be some connection between
The things she never wants to see again and
Those we lose. Is it quite coincidental?
Childhood's toys cannot speak and suffer later.
Snaps as evidence too are unimportant.
Even that uninventive frantic farewell
That one knew nothing one said now could alter
Turns up legible. Clues belong to someone,
Someone other again involved the love knots.

Still across an unpopulated ballroom
Under musical chandeliers that require
Dusting, consciousness stumbles after lights out,
Where the watery floor lies waxed and frozen
Clumsily without skates she slips and flounders,
Comes, ridiculous, to no false conclusion,
Fidgets, hesitates on the verge of the dance
Toward solitude gaping like a cupboard
In the place of the just-about-to-totter.
All things figure, the world and its abysses,
In a cabinet she pretends to know, which
Others thought to be empty, as if she cared.
Candelabra let fall their notes like snowflakes.

Ask her, what is a whatnot doing in a
Ballroom? Whose is the alibi for those hours
When pretending to sleep beside her husband
She—she too has her pointless secrets; sphinx-like
Psyche complicates what was clear as day this
Morning. Say that we only have three wishes.
One, the easiest, is recourse to silence,
Next, more difficult, is to speak precisely,
Last, implausible, are these riddling hymnals.
Each is only a way of lying and they
Do not matter a fig. So Psyche's answers,
Whether make believe, likely or true, are the
Unique oracle where love is, and why not?

BLUEBEARD'S WIFE

Impatiently she tampered with the locks,
One by one she opened all the doors;
The music boxes and the cuckoo clocks
Stopped in alarm; dust settled on the floors
Like apprehensive footsteps. Then the stores
Of silence were exposed to her soft touch:
Mute diamonds and still exquisite ores.
She had not thought the squalid world had such
Treasure to proffer, nor so easy, nor so much.

She did not listen to the hinges' groans,
Complaints in metal, warnings in the wood,
But room by room progressed from precious stones
To tears, and at each secret understood,
Exclaimed, amused, 'How simple!' or 'How good!'
As she took up some fragile, painted jar.
Throughout the palace doors and windows stood
Whether in dread or sympathy ajar
Upon a pale horizon seeming very far.

The open doors of summer afternoons,
The scented air that passes in and out
Ferrying insects, humming with the tunes
That nature sings unheard! She could not doubt
She was unseen, no one was about,
The servants all had gone—she wondered where:
The calm within was dead as that without,
And all about her breathed the stealthy air.
She knew she was alone, that no one else was there.

Now she attained the room of artifice.
Not a thing that grew there but was made:
Venetian glass that counterfeited ice
So close it seemed to melt, and green brocade,
The wind's most subtle movements in a glade.
Nothing was modern, everything was old,
And yet it was not true that they should fade
Though time and fashion dim the emerald.
Each was at once an image and a deathless mould.

Dazzled, she shut the door, but through the next
Saw greater good than any she had seen:
A window open on the sacred text
Of natural things, whose number had not been
Created or conceived, nor did they mean
Other than what they were, splendid and strange.
One leaf is like another, and between
Them all the worlds of difference range;
The world is not destroyed and does not cease to change.

The final door resisted all her strength,
No key would fit, the bars and bolts stuck fast.
But there she pried and worried, till at length
She opened it, knowing it was the last.
They hung on hooks, their finery surpassed
Each her predecessor's, in their lives
Less fortunate than she. There hung the past,
Putrid and crowned. And thinking, 'Love survives
The grave,' she stepped inside to join the other wives.

RALEIGH'S LAST VOYAGE

After the departure from the guarded quay
Under sentence of return, not 'trusty and well loved',
Though from my hands and feet the chains had been removed
My mind, my heart, my spirit were not free.
So I set out upon the sea,
The hardly serious ocean which has proved
A Circe to so many. South and west we moved
And the name of that embarkation was the Golden Vanity.

Touched by a land wind our sails of silk and cotton
Filled in the sun, fold upon hopeful fold.
Cargo hulks with nothing in the hold,
Our ships were mortgaged, more than half rotten.
Yet has disappointment long begotten
In a captive, sad, suspect and old
For a country, Eldorado, of which he has been told
A love obscured but cannot be forgotten.

But can a love so dolorous be good?
Somewhere in the doldrums fever among the men
Established the empery of boredom, fear and pain,
A reign of spleen before an age of blood,
Till waited on by sickness the commander could
Not come on deck to greet the sight of land again.
And then contrary winds and then a hurricane.
Praised be that force by which she moves the flood.

Where into the blue the brown water drops
We anchored at the Orinoco mouth
And saw on either hand a rotting growth
Of roots and broad leaves and branches and tree tops,
Tendrils twined like snakes and snakes hung down in ropes,
Bright as angels, shrill as demons both:
A fountain flowing from the gaudy south
And heaps of snow from off the mountain tops.

At San Tomé we had an embarrassing victory.
The citadel once taken proved awkward to defend
Against the besieged become besiegers. All we gained
We lost in ambush on each daily foray.
In our dreams the mine shrunk to a quarry
Like affection which becomes indifference in a friend
Or seeking hiding. There the tale should end
But I must prove the example in love's story.

For when I thought that there could be no more,
After a night of mutiny and the captain's suicide,
I learned my dear, my only son had died
In an unwatched skirmish on an unwanted shore.
Like one who sees swing to the prison door
On the whole world locking him inside
To my only listeners, cold walls, I cried,
God knows I never knew what sorrow was before.

The days grow shorter with the darkening year.
An adventurer's life is but a barren stalk.
The History of the World ends with the Prisoner's Walk
Though far and wide it seemed, and various and queer.
At the fall of the afternoon you brought me here,
To shew me the axe, the headsman and the block.
Though you torture the dumb with silence you cannot make them
    talk.
Only the dead have nothing left to fear.

THE SCREEN

The dying child reads of the lovers' flight
Behind the screen arranged about his bed.
His eyes have all the gravity of lead
And all his thoughts the clarity of a night
Whose amorous text and images affright
The innocent. Lights out, the story read,
He wonders who they were and why they fled,
Careless whether panic was their right.

On his lips, where the kiss was bred,
Breath has fastened like a parasite.
Their shut eyes from his pupils stare ahead,
They listen for the footsteps of delight.
And lost in a sensual wilderness they might
Have starved, were they not by the infant fed,
For if the unwholesome couple are his bread
And milk, he is their appetite.

Every sense, a clue however slight,
Was once with their precaution overspread.
The life they borrowed they cannot requite,
Farther than childbed they may not be led,
Nor ever known, till one or other said,
'Do not prolong it like a tedious rite.
Our steps are false and our connection light,
Trembling we trespass where we tread.'

Long after on his members fall the bright
Indulgent drops in their exertions shed.
Only in his orphanage they wed,
By anonymity accustomed quite.
Pity him? Pity them instead,
Lost in his procreation, lost from sight.
The dying child reads of the lovers' flight
Behind the screen arranged about his bed.

PATROCLUS PUTTING ON
THE ARMOUR OF ACHILLES

How clumsy he is putting on the armour of another,
His friend's, perhaps remembering how they used to arm each other,
Fitting the metal tunics to one another's breast
And setting on each other's head the helmet's bristling crest.
Now for himself illicitly he foolishly performs
Secret ceremonial with that other's arms,
Borrowed, I say stolen, for they are not his own,
On the afternoon of battle, late, trembling, and alone.

Night terminal to fighting falls on the playing field
As to his arm he fastens the giant daedal shield.
A while the game continues, a little while the host
Lost on the obscure litoral, scattered and almost
Invisible pursue the endless war with words
Jarring in the darkening air impassable to swords.

But when he steps forth from the tent where Achilles broods
Patroclus finds no foe at hand, surrounded by no gods,
Only the chill of evening strikes him to the bone
Like an arrow piercing where the armour fails to join,
And weakens his knees under the highly polished greaves.
Evening gentle elsewhere is loud on the shore, it grieves
It would seem for the deaths of heroes, their disobedient graves.

TROMPE L'OEIL

There is a way of seeing that is not seeing.
Far from the true dimension of our being
Who doubts but there is that we cannot see?
More than the naive employment of the eye
On decorated wall and ceiling,
The spirit's exercise consists in telling
Not right from wrong but rather true from false.
Looking at lies the eye sees something else,
In the pattern of the painted handkerchief
The painted pins that hold it up, and if
They yield, it cannot fall, it is not real.
Reality then is nearly what we feel
The outlines of, even as it dissolves.
Figures with better faces than ourselves
In a glass conduct their brighter lives
In chambers where reality survives
Only as long as it can fool or charm.
There at least we shall not come to harm;
Therein we and our desires belong,
Where lusts like bees perish as they sting.
Accidents that elsewhere fail to happen
Befall us there: doors that do not open,
Drawers that cannot ever be pulled out.
Disenchantment waits until we doubt
Upon the magic words, 'It all is painted.
A queer affair but hardly what we wanted,
A box containing everything but nature,
Not one unpremeditated creature,
A landscape in the manner of our dreams,
Its meaning just, it is not what it seems.'
The shadow of a fly upon the fruit
Whose suspect flesh appears substantial to it,
The deeper, broader shadow on the fly
Of the bird which it is hunted by

In the story of the still life, and
Over both the shadow of a hand
With minatory fingers seems to hover—
Will it move? or will it rest forever
On its work, a part of its creation,
The imitation of an imitation?

Round the ceiling runs a balustrade
In perspective. There the gods portrayed
As painted men and women leaning over
Laugh and kiss and talk, none whatsoever
Bored by their old immortality.
Above their heads a prospect of the sky.
The light declining on their tinted flesh
Colours with ripeness what was lately fresh
Despite the fixed meridian of the sun.
They do not seem to know their day is done,
Themselves perfected out of all ambition,
But lolling in the attitudes of passion
Sumptuously clothed or gloriously nude,
Endymion asleep, Andromeda pursued,
Ageless nymphs and coarse priapic satyrs,
They shew the features that illusion flatters
And throw from the false Olympus of the ceiling
The long, deceptive shadows cast by feeling.

There is a way of seeing that is not sight,
Like a candle lit in broad daylight,
And darkness too that is not always night.

PLAIN FARE

Night thoughts on crossing the continent by bus

How slow they are awakening, these trees,
    This earth, how late they sleep
Naked. Past the window of the bus
Where wide and nameless rivers interrupt
The plain that divided us, they stretch
Like determined sluggards muttering, 'Not Yet.'

America, the work of a magic realist,
    Make of it what you will:
The vast and apparently pointless construction
By whom—when—for what purpose begun?
The little figures beside it to give an idea of scale;
And behind, before, about like a canvas the plain.
It is disquieting to think of anyone living here,
    And the lights one sees
Rare in the darkness to unbelievable lives belong.
We too flash on their incredulity and are gone,
Cowboy and farmer buried alive in their nest,
And me sitting up all night reading *Villette*.

Sometime before dawn another stop, for breakfast—
    Country ham
And eggs—where the unfledged travellers
Wait, their faces turned from one another
In a fine balance between friend and enemy, equally nameless,
For coffee, with weary contempt and despair.

The waitress is slow, friendly but inefficient,
    The boy is impressed,
He only knows why, with these sorry unworldly exiles.
Both smile, harried and shy. It is time,
There are miles to go before morning, but no hurry.
We have ceased to believe in arrival. I ask for tea

And must decide between milk and lemon. 'Voyage'
        I used to think had
To derive from the French verb *voir* 'to see',
But blind as the best I stumble back to my seat
On the bus, take up *Villette*, switch on the overhead
Light and light yet one more cigarette.

—To be puzzled and a trifle disappointed.
        The eponymous heroine
Turns out to be a place called 'little city'
—Why not just Brussels, which obviously it is?
This is the saddest book, I think, I ever read. On
The cover it says that Charlotte Bronte,
After the death of Emily, Anne and Branwell
And before her marriage and death a year after,
'Wrote this history of lost love.'
        And when I look up
Mine is the only light still burning in the bus
Where my faceless fellow-travellers and, outside, the country
    slumber.

. . . It is day, and the lights and roadside structures have vanished.
The novel is finished and the reasons no longer exist
        For my visit. From heaven
Out of sight an audible jet
Covers in a mere hour or so
The way that I could not afford to go.

DON JUAN IN AMSTERDAM

'e tu allor li prega
Per quell' amor che i mena, e quei verranno.'
                                        —INFERNO V

This also is a place that love is known in,
This hollow land beneath a lifeless sea
Opposite to the place that he was born in,
How far it is impossible to say.
        The brackish water as I crossed
        A bridge was delicately creased
And stained and stale, like love-disordered linen.

Lovers here must meet on unsure ground
Like strangers in a circumspect hotel
Which, although luxurious and grand,
Trembles beneath their feet like earth in hell.
        Lifted on concentric gales
        Scraps of paper, leaves and gulls
Fluttered dismally aloft and groaned.

Here darkness grows and light itself decays;
Rain falls from time to time and night falls too
Upon earth's civil centre that decoys
The eternal with the promise that is now.
        There were no corners, every street
        Ran on infinite and straight,
There is no gate, no warning and no keys.

I hear a step approaching and refuse
To look aside, a while your silhouette
Persists, the fire illuminates your face
From under as you light a cigarette;
        All-knowing, arch-angelic eyes,
        Human features cut in ice—
The spark you struck at once attained the fuse.

I recognize the vanity and scorn,
The fear, the greed, in short the mask of love,
Familiar and disdainful, and I turn
About. Like children sharing what they have
     We learned in that experiment
     What the spirit's weakness meant,
The nature of the torment to be borne.

What shall I give you? What will be your price?
Your body's mine, the rich, fantastic horde
Of your embracements—angels live on praise,
Take it, it is all I can afford.
     Outside a centrifugal wind
     Sustained a freight of souls that whined
And wept along the terrible canals.

And when I close my eyes I see a ship
At anchor in the water of a bay.
I cling to that imaginary shape
Capable of taking me away
     To I do not know what ports.
     Perhaps tomorrow it departs,
Anonymous, invulnerable, free.

TRISTAN

Again the ocean rubs against the shore
And then draws back, dragging sand and stones.
Each falling wave removes a little more
Shallow flesh from the earth's enormous bones,
And white as salt, for waves of salt consist,
Gathers in with gurgles, signs and groans
What shock of meeting has not turned to mist
Nor wrench of parting left upon the sand.
Drawn by a mass that they cannot resist,
Driven by a force which they do not withstand,
Under the compulsion of the moon,
The tides exhaust their impulse on the strand
And as they ebb grind out the sort of tune
That leaves might make that whispered in a wood
Even at the breathless hour of noon
Despite the calm in which the forest stood.
A lifeless sphere, mutable and strange,
The moon compels the ocean where she would
And makes the soft, complaining billows range
Forth and back like wind-distracted grass
Or beasts transformed or in the act of change.
Upon the sand as on a pane of glass
A summer storm inscribes its track, their flight
In shells and seaweed waves describe and pass
Back into their oceanic night,
Retreating only to renew the trial
Whose issue stretches equal out of sight.
As a shadow moves across a dial,
As the sun that moves the shadow moves,
Which passion may assert without denial,
The sea resolves her love in certain grooves—
For they are thus connected, lands and seas,
And this their fond, incessant fumbling proves—
While in her heart fish glide, anemones

On a sea floor patterned like a hand
Graze like sheep and sometimes sting like bees,
Like fluid bees, and crabs run sideways and
Lung-fish gasp like lovers undersea.
The waves that make their way toward the land
And hurry on the sooner not to be
Touch the arid shore and perish there.
Waves are forms the air gives to the sea,
Clouds are shapes that water takes in air,
Aerial breakers floating soundless by
Above our heads or caught beneath us where
Their slopes, their shifting sides reflect the sky
Like winds reflected in a weather vane.

O we shall die, O we shall surely die,
Every movement makes our death more plain
And waves will break in climax on the shore
And rise and fall and fall and rise again.

THE WAVE

Suddenly it was quiet as a Sunday,
That extra day when nothing is permitted,
The first or last, whichever you prefer;
Nothing now rolled out her long-drawn sway.
The bay was like a vacant nautilus
That held in vain a secret of the sea.
Even dumb things were listening: the trees,
Sentinels of the shore, had ceased their signals,
The insects grew self-conscious and fell silent.
      Echo was dead. Dead,

Yet I think we all had the impression
That something would come to us on the water,
Music or a message or a god.
Yes, and this held all of our attention,
What was to come, whom, we must wait and see.
The afternoon was literally breathless,
Wide awake . . . Soon the promiscuous tide
As if plucked by conscience left the beach,
With a sigh the ocean fled away
      From many a strange bed.

And to be sure it was something shocking
To see the submarine groves' unguessed-at grottos
Naked, and the shame of the sea creatures
Exposed amid the wrack of rock and weed.
At the same time, as at a theatre
To warn of the beginning of a play,
There were three knocks, not loud or close together,
Distinct and distant, like that and that and that,
A reiterated hint to imitate
      The water's get-away:

As if across the empty sea came pirates
Guided by the inner vision of their kind
From the vague extremities that lie
Frozen half the time and furious,
Marked on no map or marked to be forgotten,
Realms of what use to the imagination?
Conventional antipodies of the exotic,
Without a name almost—without fuss or motive,
Without a wind through unimpeding calm
  Into the white bay.

I wanted to write it down in my diary
Then and there, this unexceptional moment,
Unique because like every other moment,
It yet had taught me what a moment was.
But even as I wished for pen and paper—
The smooth manilla sand, the ink-dark sea—
What could I say of an event where nothing happened
Save . . .? I turned to my obstinate companions,
Waiting it seemed for wave, shipwreck or ransom,
  They stood on the shore mum

Like a person standing before a door,
Listening maybe, that they fear to open,
Which will open of its own accord presently inward,
Aware of the vanity of every act.
One watched—the track of the sea, was it coming nearer?
Her back to us another, simpler, stared,
The faraway half-focused in her eye.
Some swore or prayed—I could see their lips moving.
Someone moved his hands in isolate absolution
  Or traced a Te Deum.

What happened next do I want to remember?
Perhaps we ran, perhaps we stood our ground
And the ground removed till safe and sound we arrived,
Ashamed to count ourselves, for some were missing.
Nor could we after witnesses agree
Just how the others met their martyrdom.
The seismographic report said a sea tremor,
The serious minded saw an act of God,
Both inferring further catastrophe
        Certain and sorry.

Whether those horses rode upon the wave
As some pretend, or whether the earth yawned,
As well she might in immemorial boredom,
The mess tomorrow saw upon the strand,
The common stock in trade of dogs and gulls,
The picnic drowned, dead bodies, dying fish,
Rubbish and sea things never seen before—
So the memorabilia of the flood,
God's interrupted wish-fulfillment, told
        Some of the story.

AUGUST 13, 1966

Emerging from the naked labyrinth
Into the golden habit of the day,
Glittering with sweat, a wrestler
With the sun, in his fierce palaestra,

Every drop an angel and a man,
Adept at the being that becomes a man,
You stop before the simple backdrop, look
And listen not to the abstract ocean but to me.

At our backs the breakers serially
Beat a tattoo upon the flat-bellied beach;
In our faces the minutes wait to strike and yawn;
And now the afternoon is nearly gone,
Meanwhile we sit absorbed and precious to each
Other, for the time being where we want to be.

THE WREATH

The François vase, in the Louvre, is envisaged. The story is told in Bacchylides' 17th Dithyramb, how Theseus, accompanying the last shipment of victims to Crete and challenged by Minos to prove that Poseidon was his father, dived into the sea and was received in an underwater palace by Amphytrite, who gave him a wreath of unwithering roses.

Are they setting foot
Ashore, or are they getting
On? Is it the end
Of a premeditated voyage
Or is it the beginning?
Muse, do we recognize
Among the pleasure-seekers
One to whom virtue
Once was an alternative?
I do not know who knows,

Save that one by one
The tenses are exploited,
Time itself is made
Slave to a different employment
As by a godlike labour
That could not be put off:
The something of the present
Painfully altered
To a picture of the past
Where anyone may see

As in a rear-view mirror
What he imagines best
About that other world. So

It is not possible to tell the colours of the flowers.
The porpoises that leap among the waves

Lead secret lives, shyly conspicuous.
Skill is a tyrant over seem and be.
Whose wedding chamber was a watery tomb?
Which silken shirt became a sheet of flame?
For these are only two such accidents, of many
That I could show, if it were not for time.

There was a marine wreath, a garland of unwithered roses . . .
Here they are now, forever dry and bright
Since they belonged to one who shall be nameless
From whose bones the city borrowed flesh.
Their shape is banished from the frivolous limbs
Of all the judge's victims, I mean time's,
Long since, of that half thrilled, half apprehensive cargo
Of once pubescent boys and nervous nymphs

Sentenced to be transported
With him, like Theseus,
Aboard the good ship Venus

To a terrible triumph.
Où voulez-vous aller?
The vessel is of silver,
Upon a gilded sea,
The youths and maidens are
Of lapis lazuli.

They have nothing to tell us.
Each masterpiece outlasts
The secret of its meaning
As if it ever had
A meaning. As he surfaced,
Round the ocean rang,
There crept across the water
In their wake a music
Of unutterable voices.

LADY SARA BUNBURY SACRIFICING
TO THE GRACES, BY REYNOLDS

The perfect dear whom no one blames
For her good luck and looks and breeding
Breathes from the canvas. Reynolds frames
Her in a temple, reading.

What is the book? As Sara's pale
Attention wanders from the page
Her fingers stroke the print like braille,
Her eyes engage.

Good at games? Beside her see
On a convenient pedestal
Palette and lute and embroidery,
All testimonial

To her skill in every art to which
A Bunbury may condescend,
As one of the Muses—who knows which?
Or just a friend,

A cousin, it might be, of the Graces
To whom she addresses her sacrifice:
Handsome girls with oval faces,
Straight noses and nice

Manners. Her rivals. A dainty yawn
Dimples the priestess's delicate chin.
Remark in dance on the shaven lawn
Rustics, Death and Sin.

LES YEUX DE LA TÊTE

As exercises in a foreign measure
To the ear or on the page may seem the same,
And does it matter, so the sound give pleasure?
I haunt the district under another name,
A tourist returned, sadly misdirected
By memory to the historic spot where
Once nothing happened, dark glasses reflecting
The pedestrian sun's indifferent glare.

I wear for my variety of reasons
The uniform disguise of a time and place
As much mine as anyone's. In all seasons
Lenses of necessity disgrace my face.
I grope for affection, glaucopic lover,
In bed or thinking I want to go to bed,
Blind when best to be seen. Now night shades cover
Beauties that cost, they say, the eyes of the head.

Why not? The eye is first of all a mirror,
Though not of the soul. On its bright surface swim
Whole argosies of joys. Least speaking feature,
Its objects see in it what it sees in them:
A tiny palace and a formal garden
In miniature, lawns, flowers, jewelled trees
By Fabergé, and in the midst a fountain
Whose precious drops like tear drops fill the eyes.

CLÔTURE ANNUELLE

X in August: I should not have forgotten,
I ought to have guessed that it would be so awful,
Empty, monotonous as a month of Sundays,
Yet haunted somehow like a monument
To it would be easy to say I don't know what,
Except I do: to all the other Augusts,
Equally hot or unequally overcast,
Last year and the year before the last,

When I waited, which I wasted waiting,
Wondering what else to do with time but waste it,
For the long, chaste summer to be done with, the beginning
Of intimate autumn and the promiscuous winter.
I am of those who never go away,
All the more rare, then, to find myself a stranger
In streets I thought I knew by heart, but where
The shuttered shops alone return my stare.

Life leers from every terrace and embrasure,
Tricky, inaccessible and dear.
In mid-off-season time is a temptation.
Invaders occupy the café tables
Where in the Spring we spoke to one another.
How wise you were, my dear, to go elsewhere.
Today it is clear. Search me. Our sources give
The oracle's hermetic answer, 'Live!'

NOON

Once powdered angel courtiers with short swords
And red-heeled shoes attended on the Lord's
Levée, to greet the *roi soleil*, who said,
'Sometime remember me when I am dead.'
A flutter of wings, of fans ran through the court
Provoking a spiritual lackey to retort,
'As if the bull's eye of the world could die!
Why, has not death been banished from Versailles
And never received here, even in embassy?'

That morning in the *parterre du midi*
Two peasants were apprehended gathering figs,
Male and female. Scandalized, the seraphic periwigs
Soon covered their confusion with a yawn.
Politely through the *parc du Trianon*
A *grand seigneur* escorted them, to show
Them the gates of gilt. They would not take the hint and go
Banned from the artificial wilderness
Till naked amid such shameless fancy dress
And bored by the eternal Sunday, so to speak,
The two turned to the workdays of the week
At last and left, she to spin and he to delve,
As all the clocks in paradise struck twelve.

THE TROUT

The water my prison shatters in a prism
As I leap alone the dying falls,
Cruel gasps of air, the musical chasm
Intrigue me with their broken intervals.

Deep in the noon of motionless canals
I dreamt away my pale reality
Till stirred by her immortal voice who calls
To the heights of the mountains and the depths of the sea.

I lean on air as prisoners on time
Not to let them down, my impetus
Only to the second hand sublime,
From every point of view ridiculous,

To climb the stair of stone where I was spawned,
Where ponds are oceans and the rapids give
Foretaste of the unbreathable beyond.
I try, I fall, I wriggle loose, I live

Drop by drop against the stream I am,
And in death's little cataract belong
Like Tristan to the torrent and the dam,
Liquid chamber music and still current song,

As I was laid upon the deep sea floor,
Part of the faded pattern of the carpet,
Or spilt like the sperm the kissing fish ignore
Held in each others' scales as in a net.

Yes, I exist, a memory in man
And beast and bird, a universal wish
For the watery world where life began,
And your angelic avatar, the fish:

Ambitious, ghastly, with protuberant eyes,
Or suspended like a living bathysphere,
I negotiate the steps of paradise
Leaping to measures that I cannot hear.

ENVOI

The ship is in the harbour, the fish are in the sea,
The wind is in the sails, the tide is in, and we
Are indisposed to travel, we prefer dry land,
The false, familiar face, the disappointing hand
To the stranger's clumsy touch and speculative stare.

Can you hear them singing, singing high up in the air,
The over-subtle sirens, like sphinxes, with one voice
Secretively suggesting, 'Man must make a choice.
Home is heaven and forgiveness. Abroad is simply hell.
Who would choose the ocean to inhabit, and the bitter swell?'

A VISIT

Le bonheur quel ennui! Mais l'ennui, quel bonheur!

With you the days were scarcely three hours long
Like winter days within the arctic circle
On which a brief and splendid solace shone:
What did we do on which? Let's see, on Monday
We went out, on Tuesday we stayed home
Before the imaginary fire, and read.
From time to time the cat got up and stretched and settled
On a fresh lap, encouraged by our anatomy
To resume the briefly interrupted nap
That is a cat's life. One turned a page.

How slow, how infinitely gentle then
Seemed to us the clumsy flight of time,
Like one of those birds, barnyard or extinct,
That flap from branch to branch but cannot really fly.
Each tick of the clock was noticed, weighted
Like a pulse beat at its proper value.
Thus in no time it was dinner time
And, ah soon after, time to go to bed.

Now I can't remember what we read
Or said, or even how it felt
To have you here, near, within sight and hearing,
Neglected as a treasure is neglected
By its owner, secure in his possession.
Time's deliberate pace, too, was deceptive
For even then in retrospect it flew.

What of the other days, for there were several
Sped in a variety of ways,
Spent like unreplenished capital
To the present starvation of the senses?

On one we took our borrowed bicycles
And followed a path beside the inland sea.
I said, 'Is it not like Cornwall or Devon?'
You laughed and replied, 'It might be
Were it not for all the ugliness, the highway
Nearby, the brash apartment buildings
And the widespread middle-Western platitude.'
Your kind of joke. You observed,
For it was rough, 'The waves are wearing mufflers.'
If you were a Greek you might have said,
'Underneath, the Nereids are dancing.'
And I told you how I used to come
Here alone while waiting for your visit,
In the afternoons, with an apple and a book.

It is painful to remember every morning,
Mornings too intimate almost to record,
Rich and various as a paisley scarf:
You emerging towelled from the bedroom,
And later, together in the shower, masked
In soap, slippery, lascivious as fish.
Too intimate, and yet I keep a record
Of what we did and how and when and where.
Friday you lay back upon the sofa,
Sunday I awoke within your arms,
Thursday you bestrode me like a colossus,
And it is as if in all of our embraces
The universal was made personal.

Now: now I need to stop and think a minute.
What have I left out? Oh, everything.
It is like looking at a map of or seeing from the air

A neighbourhood where once one was at home;
Like reading the menu, after, of a meal:
Is it, or in what sense was it, real?

Poets must have something else to write of
Than their own tragic thoughts and epic feelings.
But what? Will a comic interruption do?
The scramble, worthy of a bedroom farce,
When the delivery boy rang the bell, the sudden
Sinister breakdown of the telephone,
Which now, like my anxiety, seems funny.
Or your silent tears? The stories of the resistance
In which you shone with an ironic virtue
Maladroit, touchingly inferior, and wise?

The very muchness of the world disgusts me
Some times, when it comes between us two,
And suddenly I lose all appetite.
At others it is all we have together:
Like the moments on the bus, to me terrific
(You never guessed with what courage taken)
Before we said goodbye again. You proved then
How much can be included in a look,
And the fleeting sun illuminated
As it set the shining fancy of your flesh.

POINT GREY

Brought up as I was to ask of the weather
Whether it was fair or overcast,
Here, at least, it is a pretty morning,
The first fine day as I am told in months.
I took a path that led down to the beach,
Reflecting as I went on landscape, sex and weather.

I met a welcome wonderful enough
To exorcise the educated ghost
Within me. No, this country is not haunted,
Only the rain makes spectres of the mountains.

There they are, and there somehow is the problem
Not exactly of freedom or of generation
But just of living and the pain it causes.
Sometimes I think the air we breathe is mortal
And dies, trapped, in our unfeeling lungs.

Not too distant the mountains and the morning
Dropped their dim approval on the gesture
With which enthralled I greeted all this grandeur.
Beside the path, half buried in the bracken,
Stood a long-abandoned concrete bunker,
A little temple of lust, its rough walls covered
With religious frieze and votary inscription.

Personally I know no one who doesn't suffer
Some sore of guilt, and mostly bedsores, too,
Those that come from scratching where it itches
And that dangerous sympathy called prurience.
But all about release and absolution
Lie, in the waves that lap the dirty shingle
And the mountains that rise at hand above the rain.
Though I had forgotten that it could be so simple,
A beauty of sorts is nearly always within reach.

UNTITLED

Here is another poem in a picture:

at the end of the gallery, so you will see them as
you enter, Christ Crucified, the Virgin and Saint
John, attributed to a famous Flemish master.

The attribution of guilt is universal.

There is something distinctly fishy about these figures.
Literally. Streamlined and coldblooded. As weightless
as a fish might feel in water. The man of sorrows not
nailed to his cross but pinned there. Almost as if he
had no body. Nobody to suffer and depend on. No body
to depend on wood and iron and to suffer. Which heresy
pretended he did not? Nonetheless he suffers obviously,
enthroned on his gibbet, naked and erect as if he held
it up.

His mother, fainting in the arms of the disciple Jesus
loved, will never in the conceivable future fall to
earth. And this in spite of the gingerly way he holds
her as he leans slightly forward on tiptoe, his fingers
parted and outstretched as if to seize the air. His
tentative, mimic gesture of support. He does not grasp
at anything. There is no strain or effort apparent
anywhere in the composition.

She sinks down as if onto a chair, stricken by grief,
sustained in theory by love. Her hands are clasped,
her eyes are almost closed. And beneath the smooth
expressive drapery one has to infer the insubstantial
flesh. Goodness! one exclaims, What painting, a
craft in the radical sense pretentious, to suggest
what is equivocally there.

Each wears the appropriate expression like an honorary
degree: he an anthropomorphic mask of pity, she
negligently the distinction of her tears. Only the
saviour of their world wears nothing except a difficult
crown of thorns which hurts.

The cause of their distress is unconcerned. They
do not look upon him as their redeemer as yet, but
as a son and dear friend whose eccentricities have
got him into trouble. One can forgive too many and
love too much.

The birth and banquet of love look equally far away
and insignificant from here; the resurrection is also
inconceivable. Only the ignominious and painful
moment of death has any meaning now, a meaning
without a future or a past.

The background is conventional, a wall too high to
see over, too smooth to climb, draped here and there
with a red linen cloth, its folds still visible.

Beyond the wall there is a gold leaf sky.

Remember that everything is possible,
The picture, the poem and ourselves,
The blood that we see shed, the tears that we
Shed, the wall, and the anonymous cross.

TERMINAL CONVERSATION

Born to return to every strange new place,
Seeing, as the Buddha says, that you only live once,
I found myself in a great railway station
After midnight. That was late enough for me,
Though anyone who was everyone was there.
Blank terminus or furnished house? For, strange to say,
The waiting room had all the furniture of home.

It was winter, the last train had gone.
You will recognize the *mise en scène*
Familiar from too many foreign movies.
Those beside me showed no signs of caring,
And it was plain they thought of going nowhere
At that hour of the night or, already, morning.
They settled down, resident aliens,
To what they appeared to accept as the human condition,
To sleep and not to read, or to discussion
Of the trivia of their uprooted lives
In a language that, although it was not mine,
I found at once that I could understand.

What they were saying in that foreign tongue:

That emotions should be christened for their object
And not abstractly for their content. Fear and love
Would become *a certain danger* or just *you.*
Perhaps, somebody suggested, we should point
And thus avoid misunderstanding and the ills
That generally come from saying what one means.
There was a school of thought in opposition
Of course—there always is—which said
That the old names were best and meant just what they said.

Nearby some people were discussing nothing.
As far as I recall their conversation,
Some maintained that nothingness was zero
Or at least that they conceived it so,
While certain others insisted that they felt
The absence of sensation as a lack,
A positive negation, so to speak,
Dissatisfaction, disappearance, disillusion
Or even the destruction of the object,
And said that nothing equalled minus one.

All about the furniture stood, dumb,
The most expressive that I ever saw,
It had the grateful look of having been
Rescued from oblivion: those chairs
Had lived in disgrace underground for years,
And that inlaid table, too, an exile
Returned from somebody's attic déclassé
In company with the out of tune piano
And a distinctly down at heels *duchesse*.

As for the lamps: every one had started
Life as something other than a lamp,
As a typewriter, a trumpet or a doll,
And been converted, willy nilly lucifer.
Who put them there? What stranded housewife furnished
This most impersonal of places
With the heirlooms of her private fancy,
Or did I dream that they and I were there?

The station clock was keeping public time
Above our heads. A janitor
Who might have been the janitor of nowhere
Pushed his broom across the mottled pavement
Gathering cigarette ends, newspapers,
The dated detritus of a sleepless night
Into a canvas bag. I yawned, I yawn
Remembering the meaninglessness now,
The empty hours and uncomfortable faces,
The marble and mysterious conversation,
The out of place old fashioned furniture
And my secret sense that this was, where I was,
A haven however strange however new.

THE NAP

. . . and with the wingéd boy
Sporting himself in safe felicity:
Who when he hath with spoils and cruelty
Ransack'd the world, and in the woful hearts
Of many wretches set his triumphs high,
Thither resorts, and laying his sad darts
Aside, with fair Adonis plays his wanton parts.
                    SPENSER, *The Faerie Queen,* II, vi, 49

My wristwatch tells me that we've had a little nap.
        Perhaps it's stopped meantime? No, it goes,
Ticks and moves its minute hand. Upon my lap
        Catullus and *Daniel Deronda* doze.
Dreamer and reader equally, I fear to wake and snap
        The thread of their intelligent repose.
The china tea in the cup beside me is quite cold.
        Quite cold, the two extremities I hold.

With the precision of assassins the hands of the clock have crept
        Stealthily to quarter after two,
In spite of which I am unsure how long we've slept
        (For cat and book must both sleep when I do),
Nor can I remember what I was dreaming about, except
        That once again I know I dreamt of you,
Ashamed of my furtive affection, thanking the disgrace
        Of sleep wherein you have your hiding place.

No less place, to be sure, have you in waking thought,
        But there you are less vivid and you share
Their conscious character and over-complex plot
        With narratives to which you can't compare.
Exquisite structure! your doings are with such meaning fraught
        As Reason dreamt of in her *Dictionnaire.*
Awake I try your face and cannot get it clear,
        Asleep I see and touch and taste and hear.

So very near in dreams the naked body, nice
        Even when armed, and like a shield, and white;
Dark the pudenda in the midst like a device,
        The badge of bliss and blazon of delight.
There Eros practises his plays in paradise
        And member-loving Aphrodite might
Be to her Adonis for a second what she seems
        In the hall of night and hospital of dreams.

For ought I not to know the signs of the disease
        By now: what I don't have and what you are?
And see the diagnosis confirmed as it agrees
        With every previous wound and precious scar?
Fever at first is thrilling, it never fails to please,
        Only slowly do the symptoms become peculiar.
Illness is idiosyncratic: healthier to ignore
        The fact in favour of the metaphor.

Whatever science does the experiment succumbs,
        Its tools are deadly, dexterous and deep.
Each local anaesthetic altogether numbs.
        I sigh for love's suppository sleep.
Out of dismemberment the unconscious comes
        Awake to take its medicine and weep.
The dear physician does the necessary, sings
        A measure, pleasure's overture: it stings.

Antaeus when once separated from the ground
        Relaxed within the grasp of Heracles.
Above the earth he sought his mastery and found
        That he could conquer only on his knees;
As we by the laws of gravity too bound
        Savour the aftertaste of victories
In which like children caught up and tossed in sport
        We for a moment flew without support:

Until the firm familiar arms of fantasy
    Turn transparent as the windowpane,
And you as one of those, perhaps, appear to me,
    Impromptu pieces that I rehearse again
With sad darts of wit and wanton apology.
    Suddenly I feel I am in pain.
You go, I wake, Catullus stretches, everything
    Vanishes backwards, love and suffering.

TABLEAU VIVANT

Perseus on an ornamental charger,
German work, sixteenth century,
Hovering above the slumbering Medusa
Like a buzzing fly or a mosquito
On beaten, golden wings. His head averted
From her agate gaze. In his right hand
A sword, in his left a mirror.

Helmeted by night, slipshod by darkness.
Wondering where to strike. She looks asleep
As if dreaming of petrified forests,
Monumental dryads, stone leaves, stone limbs,
Or of the mate that she will never meet
Who will look into her eyes and live.

BURNT OUT

For John Miller

To come home at midnight and find everything gone
As if by disenchantment, blackened trash and rubble
In the place of your address, and to have to demand
Of a bystander, a small crowd having gathered
In partial curiosity, 'What happened?'
Is one definition of catastrophe—
Though not, for all we know, the ultimate.
Haven't we been threatened with the fire?
You may only be the first to go,
An example of that rhetoric
Which sees in flames an opportunity
To eradicate all wrongs and start afresh.

What was it you said then? What could you add,
Having searched the holocaust and salvaged
Not enough from your former life to fill a hatbox,
Hardly more than a handful of the past?
Half-a-dozen charred but, as chance would have it,
Miraculously legible paperbacks:
A Charmed Life, The Member of the Wedding,
An Introduction to the Game of Go,
The Fire Screen, Fragments of the Pre-Socratics,
Selected Tales of Edgar Allen Poe:
Out of so many why were these few elected?
How do they delineate a point of view?

The point of view of the ruined, which you know
Has been credited with simplicity,
Appears to me impossibly complex.
When one loses everything, is he
Disembarassed, free to be himself,
Or merely impoverished and out of luck?

The *Aeneid* and *Götterdämmerung*
Present the paradox in different ways:

In both a newer, maybe better world
Projected on the ruins of the old;
One, a hero modified by loss,
The other, shapeless gold redeemed from dross.

All your books and all your records burnt,
With all your worldly goods and none of mine,
The remains unrecognizable
Or worse, the works reduced to junk,
Nothing but ashes for your furniture,
And nothing but the stars above your head,
Forgive me if I envy you a little
With the jealousy of someone who has lost
Not things but beings, not property but love,
And believe me when I say, my dear,
That this disaster is nothing like the last
Which will befall you someday after all.

ANAGRAM

Oscar Fingal O'Flahertie Wills Wilde

I.e., tried for gain? How scales will fall!
Ill fared till crisis, when awe of gaol,
Law, scared off heart's wing. I lie, I loll,
Wilt. Eros fled so willing a farce. Hail!

COMMONPLACES

Places have no memory for faces.
This nowhere landscape like a windy corner,
Not the sort of spot one would have chosen
For a rendezvous, distinct, unpromising,
Metaphysical, featureless, flat, frozen,
Where anyone might feel a foreigner,
Has been somewhere one day none the less.

An accident, perhaps, such as occur
To anybody anywhere like home,
Or a meeting—who cares to recall
Of their first encounter the inauspicious setting?
Everyone, equivocal as we all
Are about sacred places, Mudville, Rome,
Texts whose true reading must remain obscure

And possibly corrupt, a palimpsest
Of names effaced or scarcely legible,
Initials which do not need to be completed,
Transitive four letter verbs that sing.
Thus literature is phrase by phrase deleted
As time decides which words are eligible
For honour, and erases all the rest.

A B. C. DIARY

For Anne and Ken Bradley

Sunday: grammar is the science of relations,
Rites of kind, visits, generations,
Regular, undistinguished, mild,
Such as I expected as a child
When games were interrupted by command,
And I, subjected to the bland
Tyranny of relatives, Who and Which,
With their distrust of the poor and envy of the rich,
Malicious gossip, symptoms, sentiment, scores,
Cursed the company of all verbal bores
And Sunday afternoon. How many years have gone
By, and again I must suppress a yawn
In the face of so much comfortable lack
Of comprehension. Why does one come back?
What have their rights and wrongs got to do with me
Whom absence temporarily set free
To eat and dress and answer or not as I pleased?
Now the demon of conformity has seized
Hold of my shrinking soul—to save, or damn?
It's enough to make me question who I am,
Yet no use asking them, they've no idea,
Though doubtless in their own eyes they appear
Unambiguous as the wedding day which breaks
Over the ubiquitous mountains. The mistakes
We made in childhood label us life-long,
Though some suppose that we went wrong
Originally in being born.
Love, whom virtues with grey hairs adorn,
Gay heart, I know that you think none of this,
Since for you existence is sufficient bliss.
For you the hours unnoticed spread their snares,
Nothing disappoints you, nothing scares,
Not even nothingness, the yawning skull
Of boredom. You discern, in the dull,

Their bright intentions, and hear in the commonplace
The inarticulate wisdom of the race,
A reservoir where all may drink their fill.
According to you, this world's a garden still,
Who live indefinitely without stimulants,
Indifferent to providence or chance.

Tuesday my embarrassed sense cannot avoid
The omnipresent titter of the void,
Like a dramatist of the *dix-septième*
For whom love and its antidote were much the same.
In theory I adhere to freedom's side,
In practice to discipline's. 'Decide!
Decide!' the compulsory chorus chants,
A chorus composed exclusively of aunts
Who taught me ennui and embarrassment
Like euthanasia were not unkindly meant,
That even when there's nothing left to say
It's essential to say something anyway,
For fear a moment slip in silence by
And silence remind us we must die.
Item: one clock brought back from Switzerland
Whose 'Cuckoo!' no one affects to understand
As a comment. Briefly undeceived
By fortune, whom our forefathers believed
A goddess, Fortuna, Tyché, Lady Luck,
Like that sarcastic record we are stuck.
Item, the Czechs, dubiously checked
Not mated, now the recent retrospect
Of liberty starts to fade upon their view.
Violence triumphs in imagination too.
Scanning the headlines' signals of distress
For the next gambit in this ghastly game of chess,
I remark that tyranny works everywhere
Just as long as its victims could care
Less, to which they impassively agree.
Later, confronted by the paradox of free
Verse, I trade my meaning for a rhyme.

Thursday. Unpunctual? No, impervious to time,
Patience is your dominating trait,
An infinite capacity for being late,
Afloat in eternity's fluid
Medium. You nicknamed me The Druid
Because of my regard for trees.
It seems several species make you sneeze,
And you detest monkey puzzles; so do I,
But if I had to live without the sky
Or water, I should not mind as much
As never to see leaves again or touch
Wood. In a wood one feels a presence
In comparison to which bipeds are peasants,
Evolution's riff-raff, without roots.
Trees, having learned to know us by our fruits,
Like defoliation, keep us at a distance.
Ecology is merely coexistence.
Conceivably tree worship must seem odd
To someone whose ancestors invented God
In a landscape the opposite of lush
With no vegetation but the burning bush.
Deserts inform the will how free it is,
While, with their limited woodland deities,
What wonder if the painted nation
Of the North profess predestination?
Hence those mutual antitheses
That in a couple cannot fail to please.
The difference that every man and woman
Boast is what we mostly have in common.
Physically and morally akin,
We seek in one another not a twin
But a transcendental object, something else,
The fascination of, not true or false,
But the equal irreconcilables of taste.
Contemporary values, haste and waste,
Translate the Augustan *Festina lente.*
Parsimony in the midst of plenty
Of the sort that soon may cost the earth
Suggests what our economy were worth.

When there are too many mouths to feed
Already, heartless bigots bid us breed
Until nature, surfeited with clients, cease
Her support. You and I do not increase.

Saturday brings me by a sententious route
To what this satire was to be about:
A homecoming and a marriage.
Far be it from an exile to disparage
Either the end or the beginning
Of that without which life would have no meaning,
But the ceremony was a joke,
And not of the kind perpetuated by folk
Lore. At the reception on the lawn they served,
Once the religious wrongs had been observed
With secular solemnity, at the most
A thimbleful of homemade wine to toast
The bride in; tea and coffee were passed later
By the bridegroom got up like a waiter
Typically in his rented tux.
The crux of these affairs is, no one fucks,
Any more than at a funeral
Mortality is alluded to at all.
Officially you'd not infer the pact
We were there to celebrate, the act
Of darkness, from our fruitcake and confetti.
The facts of life, beautiful not pretty
As my family prefer to make believe,
They hold taboo; they neither joy nor grieve
Overtly, perhaps considering emotion
Poppycock, like the Pacific Ocean,
Certainly an impertinent metaphor,
Which as neighbours they scarcely notice anymore,
So you wonder if they know it's there.
Incredulously, *O que j'aille à la mer!*
Our broad mother, not her narrow daughters,

72

Strait and inlet, domestic waters
Impregnated by the careless rivers.

Monday, belowdecks an unconscious motive quivers,
Waves slap half-heartedly against the hull;
In our wake a sympathetic gull
Follows like a ghost; vaguely through the mist
Land is apprehended to exist
As vapour condenses on the cabin window.
The horizon drops an innuendo
(So the silent ripples on a pond
Imply an event) concerning the beyond
Which opens overnight within our reach
In the changing shapes of the breakers off Long Beach.
Admiring their continual advance
I grow dizzy, as I do before the dance
I sit out after sunset on the shore:
Stars that I have never seen before
Wink at me; planets I think I recognize
Return my stare with cold, unblinking eyes.

Wednesday morning: time to mosey back
From the abyss, along the hairy track
That bisects the backbone of Vancouver Island.
The perils that befall us upon dry land
Where the precipice rises and abruptly drops
Amid gorges, torrents, rockslides, mountaintops,
Are enough to take the breath away
Temporarily. Stones seem here to stay,
To judge by their genealogy, in spite
Of erosion, earthquake, dynamite.
Names out of childhood illustrate the journey:
Nanaimo, Qualicum, Comox, Coombs, Alberni,
Mere dots in the overwhelming wilderness
On the map, the forwarding address
Of animals that elsewhere are extinct
Whose failure is intimately linked
To our success.

Friday my itinerary
Specifies an early morning ferry
To the mainland and descent of the 'Sunshine Coast'
In a shower: hereabouts almost
Three-hundred-and-sixty days of the year it rains.
This euphemism possibly explains
The hypocrisy of beautiful B.C.,
And how between the mountains and the sea
The affluent in glass houses live,
Or why, at seventeen a fugitive
From the elemental West, I sought
Salvation in the East, and found it not
Only enlightening but entertaining.
If it's childish to complain because it's raining
Childhood's an incurable complaint.
But I have learned to appreciate the faint
Deliquescence of the atmosphere,
As of the world dissolving in a tear,
That I find inevitably here.
Confronted by the everlasting rain,
My metaphysical reaction is, Again!
Reincarnation lives! since one survives
In a single life innumerable lives
Wholly or in part significant:
You'd like to understand them, but you can't.

Sunday. Obvious effects have subtle causes,
And the longest effusion ultimately pauses
For breath on the very brink of the absurd,
The future of the line and of the word
Threatened by fundamental incoherence.
Thanks to a spontaneous appearance
Which only premeditation can impart,
An accident owes everything to art.
It's not really unreasonable, is it,
If every time I pay them a visit
My family present me with a bill

Overdue and unreceipted still?
I'll pay it if it kills me, and it will.
Funny, under so much natural beauty
To discern the dull death's head of duty
Fixed in an uncompromising grin!
We resident aliens end where we begin.

PHOENIX CULPA

Adam again as his namesake nude
Awoke out of the water where his sex,
Shrunken, wrinkled to a bud,
Sprung from the fork between his sapling legs.
Eve rose to meet him. Naturally blood
Flowed in reunion; flesh like artifacts
Melted. What unimaginable good—
Family ruin, innocence in rags—
Depended on their lapse they could not know.
Then how did the revolting senses guess
That in despite of death delight would grow
Immense out of proportion to distress,
Because, though the head of state had vetoed No,
Sensibly the members voted Yes?

ON THIS ROCK

Mountains rise above us like ideas
Vague in their superior extent,
Part of the range of disillusionment
Whose arresting outline disappears
Into the circumstantial clouds that look
Like footnotes from above. What wisdom said
The mind has mountains? Imagination read
The history of the world there like a book.

Playing peek-a-boo with famous peaks
Afflicted with the vapours leaves a sense,
Frowned down upon by all that bleak immense
City of rock and ice, that men are freaks,
In the original program of creation,
Afterthoughts. Each jack pine seems a brother;
Even in lichens we perceive another
Example of our own organization,

Tenacious, patient, in a century
Growing perhaps a quarter-of-an-inch:
Glaciers do more daily, an avalanche
In minutes. The eroded immobility
Attributed to mountains is a fable,
Like the Great Divide. They move when you're not looking,
Like stars and stocks, distinctly better looking
From a distance, and chronically unstable.

SECOND THOUGHTS

How fascinating ordinary life is,
Or used to be! Selected letters tell us
Almost more than we need to know about ourselves.
Slang, the argot of affection, dates
Fatally and soon, till each stale page of gossip
Makes you want to change your name or vomit.
How could I call anybody 'doll'?
Condemn as 'cute'? or commend as 'crummy'?
Words, subjected to prolonged abuse,
Revenge themselves upon the oppressor, strike;
The phrase outraged by vulgar repetition
Returns intact to haunt its ravishers.
Yet, the sentiments were certainly sincere,
For want of a better word, the motives real;
As for the language: let its artless prattle
Not be forgotten as an object lesson
That only the most récherché style, the most affected
Can sustain the weight of time and tears and truth.

A style, that is, where anything may happen:
A sudden, not quite unforeseen conversion,
The misery of one dead-end love affair
Abandoned for another equally one-sided;
Throughout, the occasion for each thundering mistake,
The same unconscious credulity and courage.
But though incident and metaphor abound,
And the margins overflow with characters
Other than the author's, parenthetic glimpses
Of London in August, Easter in the Highlands,
Or New Year's Eve at a station buffet in East Berlin,
Even from the enigmatic postscripts
Any trace of repentance is altogether lacking.

Well, I am young, or at least I was—
As if youth could in itself extenuate
Certain failings of our former selves
Unforgivable because too often funny!
Why fuss about such widespread foolishness
When it is an all but universal fault?
These documents demonstrate if anything
The eternal adolescence of the soul,
Or that everything is mortal except life.
The nonsense that an avatar survives
Boredom, disappointment, and self-knowledge,
And being silly, giggles still at horrors,
And being human sometimes regrets his mis-spent youth!

HAPAX LEGOMENON II

Surgam et in mundo vivam —VALÉRY

Night fidgets into day, gradually
The stricken blind becomes a lambent
Parallelogram—as if it were
Yesterday? Upon the night-stand *Les*
Aides-Mémoires de Madame Truc de Chose
Open, wilted as the *Fleurs du Mal.*
Luck is getting hungry far away.
From your courtyard gurgle, are they doves,
Here, off Manhattan's dynamite row?

We who cannot sleep together lie
Higgledy-piggledy vigilant,
Counting the parachromatical
Strokes till the start of another dull
Functional day; like interior
Decorators, everybody
Prefers just such a neutral décor
To exhibit the furniture with
Which all private studies come equipped.

Who is scratching at the guestroom door?
Max: I hear his asthmatic laugh, and
Figure his horrifying mask, a
Caricature—the friendliest pug
I know—which only goes to show that
Intuition crowns the several
Senses. Different beatific
Visions we can tell by name, but Max
May perceive the beatific smell,

Or taste? or touch? Few have noted down
The *bel canto* music of the spheres;
Impressed upon the eardrums of the
Deaf (the blind would pretend, their eyeballs),
The sole figure, commonly a fugue,
To which the average aspires to
Fly. So embedded in the darkness
Like a fossil, I too entertain
Pictures of the place I want to be:

Landscape remembered as a wholly
Beloved body, here the mouth of
A river, there the foot of the hills;
An arm of the sea frames another
Neck of the woods . . . . This physical world
Abounds in arm-pits, ass-holes, navels . . . .
Bound, gagged, at the head of Death Valley
We survey a golem that distressed
Bowels of the earth did not create

Unabetted, which we may unman
By careless curiosity of
Course—illusion, if you will, and if
We will: we will, our will is in his
Peace. The creature of the air is a
Profusion, a patchwork comforter
Some in their insomnia toss off.
Which of us, survivors of ourselves,
One day will view the mayan ruin?

Whole? Herself may never hear the end
Of that ultimate *Walpurgisnacht*,
Last night, when spirits walked or flew or
Flowed to the enlightenment of flesh.
In retrospect how much might one wish
To correct or to delete! Nothing
Withstands a fanciful revision,
Yet all factual mistakes must stand
In the final draft indelible

As dawn, delectable as dream—not
That many penetrate the daylight
Stretched out cold across this crumpled sheet:
Dreams, whose cancelled versions constitute
A fair copy of experience,
Day whose lucid and pragmatic prose
Supersedes the poetry of night.
Abstract in transparent underwear
Tricks of the unconscious dissipate;

Anon, astir, my dedicated
Hosts appear for breakfast, flesh and blood—
What was I expecting? Piece by piece
We divvy up the dead body of
Our world, articulate in The Times.
Kindness in a chintzy dressing-gown
Wonders what we want to do today?
Why is this the same as everyday?
Aren't we happy just to be ourselves!

LINEAR A

For James Merrill

ἕνεκα ἀοιδῆς
ἥν νέον ἕν δέλτοισιν ἐμοῖς ἐπὶ γούνασι θῆκα

—BATRACHOMYOMACHIA

A

In the beginning is the syllable.
The rebus-writing of the universe
Puzzles our palaeographer until
He deduces it must be [free] verse.
The vatic instinct is [in]fallible.
Be[gin or be]ing, while the wo[rk is te]rse
Shew]s what a demiurge is capable
Of: a sow's [ear out of a] silken purse.

B (*Delphoi*)

The curious and desperate go [too] far.
Since the [time?] of [dawn?] contemporary
Pilgrims come to the oracular
Silence of the omphalos, the very
Spot where [*lacuna*] slew the serpent fairy
Teleph[one]—Parnassus bears the scar—
Like adolescents in the dictionary
Looking up a word for what they are.

Γ (*Olympia*)

Elements compose a landscape: queer
Haphazard ruins, some few handsome trees,
A hill, a sort of protozoic frieze
Where hieratic characters appear:
The [one] that follows and the [one] that flees,
[Indecent details delicately clear]
With possibly a Mourning Siren here,
And here, an Impersonation of the Breeze.

Δ (*Bassai*)

Apollo turns [his back upon] the world.
Faced with the uncomely mountainside,
No wonder he's so beautifully preserved,
Ageless [mythological] and blind.
The other immortals, who are More Than Kind,
Say it was no less than he deserved
Because of the anthropo[morphic pride
Naturally incarnate in the word].

E

'Mind of Apollo'—whatever that may be!
Glazed, hermetic as a casserole.
Know [*thyself,*] *Nothing* [*in excess*], a whole
Treatise on the single letter E:
E[very] e[mpty-day] e[piphany].
Inspiration signifies the sole
Undisputed world authority,
Inventor of cosmetics and the soul.

F

Eternal youth? Eternal [middle]age
Lies [in the gift] of the Olympians
Whose ever-during date is yesterday.
What if their make-up were [every]man's?
What would you expect [a god] to say?
A commonplace is sacred if it scans.
The Alph[abet] meanders on the page,
Spondaic as all rivers: *panta rhei.*

Z

Beneath the Epicure the silly herd
Browses on theatrically curved
Natural terraces the valley wide.
Visiting Arcadia you find
The infrastructure of the underworld
Which, hypnotized by his bucolic guide,
The [Ptolemaic] cosmonaut observed,
Apollo out of sight and out of mind.

H (*Pylos*)

What a place to start looking for a father!
At night [the little port is full of life—
What passes [for it in the guidebook, rather.
The fort down the coast, marked with fork and knife,
Serves [heroes] roasted whole. A little farther
Out there squats the unrepentant [wife
Re]domesticated after the long [p]other
Of controversy, heavenly trouble and strife.

Θ (*Gytheion*)

[Once you've seen one rape you've seen them all.]
More than the noise, the smell, the dirt, the jetty,
Its customers define a port of call.
Traditionally amid a flutter of amoretti
Hence they embarqued for Asia. At landfall,
Regretfully foreseeing how the petty
Warlords she had met in her husband's hall
Would take the snub, she warned her friend [. 'Forget,' he

I

Said, ']about the details of the trip
Arranged by Eros Tours. The naughty boy
In person is the pilot of this ship,
The hours, her deckhands, the figurehead is joy.
Ours is a bitter elixir, one sip
Of it sufficient to destroy
A civilization.['] Biting her pretty lip,
Helen fretted all the way to [Troy.

K (*Mistra*)

You were our ruin: had you withstood
The sultan another century or so,
Classical antiquity would
Have endured until today[?] As empires go,
Yours went.] But was it ever any good
After all?] itself an afterglow
Whose intensity [mis]understood
A duration [we] shall never know[?]

Λ

The Palace of the Despots on your left;
Right, the Mistress of the Universe.
[Eponymous Mistra!] bathykolpic cleft
Of Taÿgetus] superstitious nurse
Of the Renaissance; in deed, the Turk was worse.
Either [too little] or [too much] is left
Of frescoes mysteriously bereft
Of charm: Pantanassa had the curse.

M (*Mycene*)

What the cost of living must have been!
K[lytaemestra,] A[gamemnon]—tit for tat:
For all the difference between
Them, it wasn't long the royal fat
Was in the fire that licks the tablet clean.
But all the finest families come to that:
Late dynastic gold-masked king and queen
Under one stupendous beehive hat.

N (*Athens*)

Atop its wobbly acropolis,
A doll's house, Doric cheek by Roman jowl,
Immortal toy today in mortal dis-
repair, its facade disfigured by the foul
Heirs of the [X]tian metropolis
Whose modern mode of music is a howl,
The Parthenon [abandoned by Her owl?]
Grandstands above time's backward abyss.

Ξ

Surreptitious as a revelation,
Open-handed, [*Hydra*-]headed light
Penetrates the present; yet the sun
Is like a lover who stays out all night.
A discothèque, the beach, some shops and bars,
An architecture all of building blocks,
The absence, while it lasts, of motorcars,
The lucubrations of the native cocks [. . .]

Ο

Affront a uniform, push-over pilgrim
Tired, as who isn't? of his kind
Enough to make him wish to stay a week
Away from the exhaust and noise of Athens,
Looking for the original of hymn
And idyll which he somehow failed to find
Where they were so signally to seek,
Back in the [itchy] world of [aller]gens.

Π (*Ramnous*)

Puerile, to prevent a deux-chevaux
In the middle of nowhere [Her established site],
Where, while we attended rescue, night
[Gradual as Nemesis, and slow]
Overtook us, till at last the light
Expected shone, and we were free to go.
Adrastia—'inevitable'—slight
Her Nastiness, and She will let you know.

P

Who's boss? [Who pares the wants?] A dangerous,
In fact a *femme fatale*, whose promise, 'Late,
But never Never!' still confounds with fuss
Who think they can control their own estate.
Providence, some times praeposterous,
At others [un]predictable as Fate,
Felicitates occasionally us.
They always serve Her turns who only wait.

Σ

From shame to [guilt, from guilt to what?] success?
Dithers our mythopoeic gyroscope
Which measures [lackaday] a little less.
How can we [un]do [ourselves un]less
Eternity provide sufficient rope?
As [whatchamacallit] slithers down the slope
Of [thingamajig], giddy amid the mess
Who think they glimpse the rusty anchor, Hope.

T

Prospects: better than they look at first.
From the sea the land seems [blank] and brown.
Turning a dull profile to the town
It shows the Mediterranean its worst,
A picture of inhospitable thirst*
That greets all comers with a Parian frown;
But just as they expect to be let down
The peripatetic pattern is reversed.

As Archilochus was the first to own.

Υ

A microcosm: the ideal size.
Elsewhere sirens [sing] and [harpies] seize.
Exile's an untidy paradise,
Chryselephantine island, sapphire seas,
A parish visited by butterflies,
Dolphins, donkeys, pleasure-seekers, bees,
Where those who hold [our] knitting on [their] knees
Dropped a stitch in [lieu of] a surprise.

Φ

Inhuman[kindness cannot be forgiven.
Who can forgive what they don't understand?
Difficult to bear, the gifts of heaven,
Notoriously on the other hand.
Whatever god you ask, the odds are even
You will get rather more than you demand.
Welcome in the spirit they were given
The] beauties [of the god-forsaken land.

X

It is the archaeological view
That holds that [life] is short and [art] is long,
Its partisans the sometime happy few
Who know to whom the particles belong.
Yet both the ancient tongues I thought I knew
Prove in the mouth irrelevant or wrong,
And in their place I have to offer you
These *comprimés* of analgesic song.

Ψ

Here are the] tablets[. Take one a day
[Mornings before you break your fast,]
[Or bedtimes by the handful. Any way]
[The doctor orders, even first to last.]
In[decipherable pre]scription: [put away
[The pain of the present, the pleasure of the past.]
[Symptoms don't make anybody gay.]
[Set in your ways? The rule is hard and fast.]

Ω

The dippy pen when pushed to a reply:
Your drunken lover's notes are [sour] mash.
[Te]dium, te[dium], emphatically I
Take for iam[boi] anapaestic trash.
Icarus, pretender to the sky,
Ended in the water with a splash.
When hippies come to supper give them hash:
Simple, in [geo]metric terms, as π.

ACRE

The Cyclopean walls are tumbledown,
The narrow streets, dirty and confused.
The famous port washes the vacant quay
(Vacant except for dust and melon rinds)
Like dishwater: argosies of garbage
Nibbled by fish decorate the surface.

This is Acre, built by What's-His-Name,
Mentioned in the Tel Amarna tablets;
Once called, like the fishy restaurant where we ate
An Alexandrian luncheon, Ptolemais,
Then, sycophantically, Colonia Caesaris Claudii;
Fought over by the crazy crusaders, taken
By, among others, Richard Coeur de Lion,
And entered in premature triumph by an Anglican
Archbishop come all that way to see its fall.
The Teutonic Knights, of sinister memory, were started
Here. Here the Knights of St John had their hospital.

Would you like to climb the thirteenth-century tower
For a panorama of poverty-stricken streets,
Mean mosques, and, when you reach the top, the sea?
This city, which appears to have been founded by sand fleas,
Boasts the cheapest, or most comparatively inexpensive
Bazaar in the East, where the knowing traveller
May purchase at a reasonable rate
Native wares of aluminium and plastic.
Flies like tourist guides are everywhere,
The sight of the sook induces diarrhea,
Even the shopkeepers' 'Welcome, Mister' lacks the vigour
Of delivery you get in David Street.

Descend the corkscrew staircase, *Fuyons ces lieux*
Saints. Quitting the Mosque we fight our way
Out of the filthy labyrinth to the harbour,
Where the horrible children that pursued us
Hitherto are diverted by a bird,
A wounded seagull one of them has caught
By the wing, and of which they will make
First sport, then supper. Lady Hester Stanhope
Might have bought the bird and wrung its neck.
Rejecting all such missionary gestures—
Bored and itchy, who are we to judge?—
We drive away secure in our rented Hertz.

LETTER TO SHADOW

Bit by bit, as in a picture puzzle,
    The prospect of this present disappears
Into that panorama of the past.
    Dotted with illegible menhirs
The flat and sentimental landscape that
    You read as a romance, the prose plateau
Of fancy half-developed like a snapshot
    Lies printed with the alphabet of shadow.

From left to right, an amphisbaenic sense,
    Black on white, a sensuous photograph
Of a too formal period, death's sentence
    Closing life's emotional paragraph,
Tuneless, tasteless, without text or tincture,
    (N.B., hieroglyphics have no tenses)
Lucid and superficial cynosure,
    Literature is all a letter says.

What alternative to tell a vision?
    So doting on the idiotical light
Within's like staring at the sun: one
    Sees no more than if he looked at midnight . . .
Midday composes shortest, sharpest shade,
    Underlining objects in italics
On our universal page whose man-made
    Margins a little intuition fix

In the dictionary mirror.
    Seeing if you nab one you feel nothing,
Imitation, neither less nor more,
    Its shadow is the name of anything,
The mystery whereby sight were baffled,
    Sacrament and written character,
Labarum above the battlefield
    Of words, which always was a massacre.

WHAT'S HIS FACE

The god that is leaving me perhaps has left
Already; bereft of his presence I breathe lighter.
What was his name? Apollo, Eros, Zeus,
As he pretends? Or one of their attendants?
By turns appalling, erotic, zoomorphic,
He might have been some petty local demon,
His divinity unrecognized by the tribe next door,
His attributes demonic to a fault,
Ithyphallic, pushy, mischievous,
Totally undependable, adept
At deceit while he denies he led you on:
Impalpable, incomprehensible . . .
He appeared in the flesh—what? half-a-dozen times?
Smiling his cryptic, unforgiving smile,
Saying little, glimpsed in intervals
Of sleep or at a distance, domestic idol
Destructive of peace and quiet. Now he's gone
Life is private again, desecrated, dull,
Without his infrequent fraudulent manifestations,
Without his unconvincing oracles.
His image, which was cast in terra cotta
And clumsily, though not unattractively, modelled,
Smashed, and his untidy shrine abandoned,
Having given nothing to his votary
Has he turned his face toward the dawn?
Is he visiting with the Hyperboreans? God
Forgive me, what made me think he was a god?

VOWEL MOVEMENTS

Take a statement, the same as yesterday's dictation:
  Lately pain has been there waiting when I awake.
Creative despair and failure have made their patient.
  Anyway, I'm afraid I have nothing to say.
Those crazy phrases I desecrated the paper
  With against the grain . . . Taste has turned away her face
Temporarily, like a hasty, ill-paid waitress
  At table, barely capable but very vague.
Mistaken praise and blame degrade profane and sacred
  Places so strange you may not even know their names.
Vacant the gymnasium where words once played naked
  Amazing games that always used to end in mate.

Better, then, the effort than preterite perfection,
  I guess. Indeed, I envy the eminent dead
The special effects I am ready to inherit
  Less than their sentiments and impenitent sense
Of aesthetic gesture. Unpleasant and pretentious,
  The Western hemisphere has plenty to forget.
The mess men might yet make of themselves, given present
  Events! Are many content to accept the best?
Precious as sex is, flesh, perennially wretched,
  Begs the bread of heaven, blessing nevertheless
The unexpected sender's address on a letter.
  Every breathless sentence says not yet to death.

The past cannot matter except as an abstraction,
  A flattering caricature of happy lands
Wherein many a grand, imaginary castle
  In fact turns out to be a tourist trap at last,
A vast palace that adrastic phantoms inhabit.
  Maps of madness, characteristically blank,
Ask vatic questions, exact a magic answer:
  The family photograph album at a glance,

Granny, Dad, Aunt Sally, that dissatisfied madame
    Who manages passion's incalculable acts,
Paris, everyman's romantic trash and tarry—
    Abracadabra, and the vanished cast comes back!

If civilization isn't a silly gimmick,
    Is it the wit to wish, the will to make it stick?
The mathematical vision which built this system
    Figures'the width of a minute within an inch.
Primitive physics, a sophisticated fiction,
    Insists that in principle everything is fixed.
Visitors picnic amid pretty *Chichèn Itzá*
    With its sacrificial pit, artificial hills
And cricket pitch wherein the winner is the victim.
    To think an instinct like iniquity exists!
Hidden riches fill big individual middens;
    In the Wizard's Pyramid little lizards live.

Specious sweets we reach for eagerly with Eve's evil
    Greed recede like the fleeting details of a dream.
It seems that we have been a brief season in Eden:
    Chic unreal estates where immediately green
Trees repeated in completely meaningless series
    Briefly yield to the weaker tyranny of weeds
Even as we seek relief in a secret clearing.
    Prehistory can be too recent; need we read
These steles' queried speech? Here undefeated peoples
    Experienced deceit; here scenes of deepest grief
Teach us to weep the cheap and easy tears of reason;
    Here the sea of being sleeps, a period peace.

Frustration, fuss, and lust are love's unlucky colours.
    Thunderstruck, the muscular monuments look dumb.
Judged by the numbers that once flourished in the jungle
    In hundreds of miles of dull undercover scrub,
Unless somebody was insufferably ugly
    Mistrust of one another must be in the blood.

Unsuccess in a dozen tough struggles instructs us
    Justice is a mother-fucker. Suffering's fun
For a month, but in a millenium no wonder
    One becomes somewhat disgusted. Unsubtle skull,
The mysteries of dust are nothing to live up to.
    Insulted by a touch, one mutters, 'Summer sucks.'

Undone by the siesta and by sudden showers,
    Is it uncomfortable in the hungry South?
Now cowed by Kulkulkan's geometrical scowl,
    Now wowed by the classic brown faces in a crowd,
You falter at mounds memorial to a thousand
    Bleeding hearts in a single holiday cut out,
Submitted to the sun, insatiable flesh-flower
    Of the universe, all-devouring powerhouse,
Confounded by our sound of pronounceable vowels.
    Myths, as the guidebook says, are handed down by mouth.
Though mood and voice and person, gender, tense, and number
    Predicate a verb, its cases explain a noun:

Proper noun or pronoun, indubitably human,
    Whose beautiful excuse is usually youth
Doomed to the brutal usufructu of the future,
    Consumed by the illusions of jejune amours.
You used to choose the rules with superfluous humour,
    Tuned to the influential movements of the moon
Whose smooth, translucent route through roofless rooms illumines
    From dewy moonrise unto lunar afternoon
Tulum and its improvements, tumulus and ruins,
    Poorly reproduced, a too crudely stupid view.
Who knew nude truth from rumour, amusement from music
    Soon would prove a fool. Beauty, useless, is a wound.

On and off; the impossible is honour's motto,
    Monotony the awful drawback of my song.
What was lost was often all we had got in common,
    Our quasi-comic quandary depended on

Qu'en dirai-je? chronic, colossal hypochondry,
    Neurotic complication or hypnotic calm.
Gods begotten of loss, not bronze nor terra cotta,
    Haunt the province of law, of cause and conscious wrong.
Following the Long Count a lot has been forgotten:
    Positive nonsense, fraud, false plots and hollow talk,
Soporific concepts toppled by fall or conquest,
    The cosmos as a model watch that wants to stop.

At any moment the doors of the soul may open
    And those reproachful ghosts invoked from the remote
Coasts of tomorrow begin to impose the order
    Of bone and trophy, home and the odour of smoke.
O mornings that broke on the slopes of cold volcanos,
    Almost frozen, golden and old-rose, like a scroll
Slowly unfolded, or a brocade robe thrown over
    The throne of the mountains, cloaking their cones in snow!
Hope, an emotion swollen by every omen,
    No psychotrope, only a semiprecious stone,
Topaz or opal, adorns the close of the strophe.
    Woe wrote these notes in a code also known as prose.

Ode: this leafy, streamless land where coy waters loiter
    Under the embroidered soil, subterfluous coin
Of another culture destroyed by lack of moisture,
    Spoiled by the unavoidable poison of choice.
Archaeological lawyers exploit the foibles
    Of a royalty that in time joined *hoi polloi:*
History's unemployed, geography's anointed,
   Unlike the orchids of the forests, spin and toil.
Imperfectly convinced of final disappointment,
    Persuaded of the possibility of joy,
Pen poised for the pointless impressions of those voices
    That boil up like bubbles on the face of the void,

Finally I try to define why divine silence
    Underlies the tidy designs of paradise.
Priceless as the insights of the inspired psyche,
    Blind, violent as a geyser, right as a rhyme,
Fine ideas likely to undermine the idle
    Mind divided between the types of fire and ice,
'Highly stylized' politely describes the bright eyesores
    Shining like diamonds or rhinestones in the night sky,
 Lifelike, provided life survives its vital cycle
    And the tireless indictment of time's diatribe,
While mankind, sightless, frightened, like a child in twilight,
    Dies of the devices it was enlightened by.

    Amazing games that always used to end in mate!
Precious as sex is, flesh, perennially wretched,
    In fact turns out to be a tourist trap at last.
The mathematical vision which built this system
    Of the universe, all-devouring powerhouse,
(The mysteries of dust are nothing to live up to!)
    Briefly yields to the weaker tyranny of weeds.
You used to choose the rules with superfluous humour:
    Monotony, the awful drawback of my song,
Slowly unfolded, like a brocade robe thrown over.
    Persuaded of the possibility of joy,
Finally I tried to define why divine silence . . .

PARAPHRASE

After a certain age your body ceases
To be an interesting topic, and becomes
Another object, of some utility until
In the end of course it is no use at all,
Not even to its former owner and companion;
On the dirty beach an empty
Shell or bottle, an abandoned home
Uninhabitable by the tenant
To whom it was originally attached;
A machine irreparably idle . . .?

Not necessarily,
Seeing the body must remain its subject,
Itself at once both predicate and verb,
An organic calculator
Living a life of sorts unprogrammed by the mind,
Transmitting messages nobody it thinks will understand,
Many of which are intercepted by the reader,
Receiving in return a few laconic orders—
O that its every wish were our command.

AETATE XXXIX

Infrequently we feel the need
To celebrate our being here.
As the unfunny years succeed
Each other at increasing speed
Easy reasons disappear
Eagerly to persevere,

Yet we do, beyond a doubt
Programmed by a will to live
Which seems to offer no way out.
Baffled what it's all about,
Who can figure or forgive
That idiot imperative?

Reality is all there is,
Unfortunately, nothing else
Approximately satisfies
Our appetite for fiction, *viz*.
The metaphysical impulse
That develops true from false.

No sacred save in the profane.
Daily trivia erase
All trace of the transcendent: vain
As well as graceless to complain.
Praise falls silent face to face
With everything that is the case.

Body functions like a clock,
A clepsydra, drop by drop
Exhausting its spasmodic stock
Of water, till a modest shock
Brings the clockwork to a stop
And the sodden contents drop

Into earth's unimpatient hand
As if astonished—that is all?
What was there to understand?
Life evaporates in sand,
A sporadic waterfall,
Squandered, lost, beyond recall.

MY OPTICS

Innocently then they
Framed the world in plastic
Imitation tortoise
Shell which at eleven
Knowing nothing better
I took for the real thing.
Still at nearly thirty-
Nine the limits of my
Outlook are determined
By their necessary
Focal intervention:

Spectacles, perspectives
Edged by sentimental
Temples in repair, their
Extraordinary
Centres, convex crystal
Visionary wells that
Entertain the sunlight:
Fountain, mask or window,
Temporary mirrors
Endlessly reflecting
Heaven's unexpected
Entrances and exits.

Ithyphallic, dactyl,
Iambelegiac,
Such cosmetic measures
Seem preservatives or
Spices to embalm the
Evanescent sentence.
Metrical devices

With corrective lenses
Bring the phrase in focus.
Form is recognition
Of an underlying
Symmetry in something.

Physical perfection
Was a shibboleth for
Unsophisticated,
Acned adolescence,
Faces without any
Blemish or expression,
Specs or spots or braces.
Now a new aesthetic
Welcomes affectation
In embellished features;
Status symbol, fetish,
Four eyes are in fashion.

Often in the act of
Sex they are abandoned.
Balanced at the bedside
See our twin prescriptions
Gleam, a pair of glasses
Disaffected, empty,
Drained of speculation.
Touchingly myopic,
Lovers, twenty, forty,
Put their faith in contacts.
(Parenthetically
Feeling is believing.)

Everything without them
Melts and runs together.
Wanting an horizon
Foreground grows important
Out of all proportion;
From the middle distance
Detail is omitted.
So in daily life your
Future blurs, uncertain,
Past retreats, forgotten,
Leaving nothing but an
Undistinguished present.

FRANKENSTEIN'S FAREWELL

Starved for electricity, it started
Twitching, the carnal statue stirred
Erect; before the process was reversed
'Beautiful' emerged as its first word.
Then in the rude laboratory where
It was delivered by a thunderstorm,
A plagiarized, imperfect form
Intimating sex and personhood,
Warm from the sarcophagus, it stood:

Completed like a patchwork, piece by piece,
Improvised grotesque that wept and smiled
With the idiotic courage
And inadvertence of a child;
Imaginative miscarriage
Whose conception seemed a slap
At the rule of nature, from whose sleep
It was inveigled by a slip
Of the pen, my accidental masterpiece!

Limbs that, sad and flaccid in repose,
Manipulative fingers taught to speak
Their universal lingo, specious, weak,
And yet with the distinction of a rose;
Obsidian eyes that half disclose
A vision of existence heartless, bleak
As an extermination camp—from those
Odd elements this superlative physique
Arose, at once eclectic and unique.

(Should I have foreseen he'd lose his looks,
As all creatures must what few they have?
No longer it, he never lost his look
Of devotion and reproach; while I kept mine,
An appearance truth cannot deprave.
But how unlike a mesmerist to love
The rescued flesh, the seamy skin
Instead of that which animated them,
Hypothetically, within!)

Forward as a schoolboy, backward as a bride,
He hid inside the wardrobe to deride
My habits, the amenities that hide
The terror that we feel of the outside.
Now I initiate the suicide
Of science, whose conclusions I tried—
A failure? Let experiment decide.
Remember the creator's hands are tied;
Curiosity is never satisfied.

Perhaps one ought to hate what one has made,
Like mankind, modelled from the mud
Of myth, his mate from borrowed bone and blood,
And that last monstrosity, a marriage
For material advantage?
What is a caricature, to criticize
Its author, or a body, to disparage
A resurrection framed as a surprise?
Unnatural Adam,

Echo and her boyfriend both,
Turning dumbly from the unresponsive
Surface, and fixing an infatuated
Gaze on this compromised original,
At last a speaking likeness:

'Tantalized and badgered into life
Second-hand, I dreamt of death,
As if that were an alternative!
I died so often I cannot again,
I cannot die, although my beauty can,
And with it every smidgin of affection
Philanthropist professed for man,
No immortal paragon but an
Abortion stinking of the grave.'

Your past, a compass needle pointing North,
Brought us to this gothic precipice
To be buried by forgiveness. With a kiss
We open the ridiculous abyss.

To be continued. Might one write a novel
Using no other characters but us,
You the second person ambiguous
And me a fascinated first,
With him and it diminished thirds
Present like an unimportant chorus
As a background to the action
Contributing a moral or a curse,
After the catastrophe of course!

ARRONDISSEMENTS

For A B

T'introduire dans mon histoire . . .

I^e *Palais Royal*

A foreign city in a foreign language:
Errors you will find your way around
Less by misconstruction of an image
Idiomatic as the underground
Than by reference to the lost and found
Out-of-date semantic luggage
And archaic sentimental slang which
Used to mean so much. Beware of the sound,
Volumes of experience rebound,
Sense can take care of itself. Abandoned baggage,
I sought to celebrate you, not confound;
Apart from the smarts you brought me, *grand dommage,*
A throne's stowaway, you still astound
The razor's edge dividing youth from age.

IIe *Bibliothèque Nationale*

'Nothing but a pack of cards' obscurely comments
Dimbulb, whose enlightenment must prove
A catalogue of incandescent moments—
Years shrunk to days, hours hung like months—
That categorically survive
Oblivion in a cross-indexed grave
With other mortal meantimes, to achieve
The brazen afterlife of monuments.
This mental midden, almost as immense
As the world it was the wonder of,
Which it can't comprehend but complements,
Does it explain what evidence we have,
An ennui ingenuity augments,
Cruising the pages of the treasure-trove?

IIIe *Arts et Métiers*

There are shady purlieus no one wanders
Except in speculation, ways
Affected by perpetual pretenders,
Amateur meanders that amaze
The tourist who professionally blunders
Into labyrinths through which no stranger strays
Prepared. What lies or (literally) lays
Behind the glazed pentameters of windows
With their drawn, blind, introspective gaze,
The passer-by pedestrianly wonders,
Besides florid wallpaper and bidets?
The encyclopaedic street surrenders
Secrets sometimes lost in paraphrase:
Moods, tenses, persons, numbers, genders.

IVe *Quai d'Anjou*

Superficially the envelope
Sports the legend, *Addressee Unknown*:
The familiar, arbitrary shape
Of the letters seems strange at the same
Time you recognize them as your own,
Returned to Sender. Stereotype,
Signature or pseudonym,
The ultimate enigma is your name.
Too trivial for the microscope,
Repetitious as the gramophone,
The recycled syllables escape
The statement you were brash enough to sign
Forever yours, the sort of tripe
One writes when one is twenty-one.

Ve *Quartier Latin*

Jardin des Plaintes, Pandémonium, Coup de Grâce:
Starred sites we circled all night long,
Apart from a crepuscular embrace
Incommunicado. Being young,
With other clubs invited to belong
To, nationality, gender, class,
Impressed us then as a disgrace,
Almost an unconscionable wrong,
To which, not quite unconsciously, we clung
As if for life, in spite, or just in case,
Like friendship, unexpected as a song
Before sunrise in a silent place,
Or the comforts of our mother tongue
Overheard on some café *terrasse*.

VIe *Institut Français*

Six flights below my balcony the traffic
Percolates the narrow rue de Seine,
At the same time tepid and terrific,
Uninteresting and obscene.
The footstep on the stair of a petrific
Visitor unnaturally soon
Arrests the contemplation of specific
Images that persecute the sane.
Again today deciphers pornographic
Night's incomprehensible design,
Every superstitious hieroglyphic
Reified by an explicit sun,
Shades uncensored by the soporific
Darkness of which dreams are partisan.

VIIe *Chambre des Députés*

Overshadowed by the Ministry of War,
We shared an absurdly furnished flat,
Dubious *Empire* and *Directoire*,
With an early modern bathroom, that
Winter, until the tasteless coup d'état
Of Spring, insurgent in silk underwear.
Folly, female, fortyish and fat,
Found me a companionable if queer
Cohabitant of her cosy habitat,
A ménage of inconvenience where
We lived like dog and wife and man and cat,
Compatible antagonists aware
Of a temporary tit-for-tat,
Like it was, or rather, as it were.

VIIIe *Elysée*

Anatomy of a mistake,
The structure of affairs is uniform,
Part of the pathological mystique
To which romantic accidents conform.
Infatuation's formidable physique
And infant physiognomy confirm
The pattern of attraction, one unique
To fantasy's Elysium.
Thus enfranchised of that funny farm,
Unfortunate affection seems a freak
Of feeling, the inevitable form
That fatal fascination has to take.
How often out of nightmare do we wake
Beside the one whom we were fleeing from?

IXe *Opéra*

Tedious the intervals of living
Between the acts, etc.,
Clichés as distinct from moving
Parts depicted by the camera,
Interludes in an indulgent era
Dissipated by the disapproving
Scrutiny of tomorrow
Which will, I fear, be unforgiving;
Then delinquent evening arriving
Splendid in her twinkling tiara,
An hour late, delayed by daylight saving,
A dusky demimondaine with an aura
Of the Belle Epoque, surviving
As a backdrop to the opera.

Xe *Gare du Nord*

Haunted by arrivals and departures,
The desperate farewell of handkerchiefs,
This dingy greenhouse architecture nurtures
An exotic growth of greetings, griefs
And brief encounters under iron arches
Overlooked by smutty petroglyphs.
Having said goodbye to make-beliefs
And all a single backward glance can purchase,
Through the unsympathetic crowd one searches
Among reunions, tears and tiffs
Unfamiliarity that tortures
The traveller with interminable ifs
For those extraordinary features
Familiarity enfeoffs.

XIe *Saint Ambroise*

Never underestimate the slogans
Scribbled overnight in public places—
Ambrose Go Home! Power to the Pagans—
Nor the civilization that defaces
These legends fabulous as dragons,
Paleskin texts with redface prefaces,
Profane initials, sacred organs
Erased to make way for an oasis
Paradise of perfect paragons
Whose nomenclature graphically embraces
Dead ends and picturesque parentheses,
Ruinous beginnings that seemed bargains
Once, the revolutionary faces
Of those who let byegones be byegones.

XIIe *Porte de Vincennes*

Irradiating like a dull penumbra
The suburbs of the citadel of light,
Detours without character or number
Advertise contemporary blight;
Here history, inimical to slumber,
Held up the royal nincompoop in flight
Just because she could not disencumber
Herself of her ancestral appetite.
The autumn of *le feu régime,* remember?
The eve of what we came to call The Fright,
The first Brumaire—is that November?—
Alias All Hallows' Night,
With the Sun King an extinguished ember,
And evergreens in periwigs of white.

XIIIe *Salpetrière*

The thirteenth returns—yet it is the first
Time we proximately failed to meet
Across the gap our ages made reversed,
That post meridian I watched you beat
Time at your open window, indiscreet
As innocence incongruously cursed
With a precocious portion of man's meat.
In solitary vice immensely versed,
I kept time while puberty rehearsed
The age-old ritual of self-defeat,
Pricking the tumescent bubble till it burst,
An agon adolescence can repeat
Ad nauseam, while sympathy, in heat,
Next door to the fountain dies of thirst.

XIVe *Observatoire*

Obvious from the Observatory,
After the abdication of the moon
Heaven explicates a bedtime story
Full of incident and interest, humane
Like anything significant to man,
The everlasting, transitory
Celestial phenomenon
In all its superannuated glory,
A *roman fleuve* that one is always sorry
To see abridged by dawn. The stars remain
Secure in their orbits, never in a hurry,
Worlds superior to yours and mine,
Dispassionate, explanatory,
Suggesting more than they can ever mean.

XVe *Vaugirard*

Tabula rasa, fair and vacant page,
Impenetrable open book unlined
By the ineradicable afterthoughts of age,
Inane impressions that outrage
The paper void its blankness can't defend,
What an idea, to be defined
According to the petty average
And calculated meanness of mankind,
Catalogued, confined
Captive in the cage,
Cosily conventional, of kind,
A jejune personage
Whose very emptiness may yet engage
The spirit when the flesh is out of mind.

XVIe *Muette*

In eccentric circles memory
Like a longplaying record crazily revolves
Until the trivial, terminal melody
Abrupts, its lifelong dissonance dissolves
Into the operative gears and valves
Of time's Edwardian machinery.
Song concocts some problems that it solves
Often with an astonished Q.E.D.,
A rational equation that involves
Real variables, you and me,
Coefficient and unequal halves,
Imaginary numerals, a to b,
The coordinate conjunction of our selves
Or the cyphers that we used to be.

XVIIe *Ternes*

Absence is a type of convalescence.
Committed to this gothic hospital
Where life has been protracted to a sentence
Episodic, periodical
As a phantom cast upon a wall,
Grotesque, distorted, menacing, immense
Out of all proportion to the small
Object that caused it, I begin to sense
The possibility of being well,
Eventual recuperation from a spell
Baneful mainly in the present tense.
Practising your absence as a penance,
Like an ascetic anticipating hell,
I come to appreciate the presence
Of the sacrament that says it all.

XVIIIe *Montmartre*

Kindness is for mortals, only they,
In this world reluctantly at home,
Find it an amazing place to stay,
Sympathetic as a rented room
Where one is here tomorrow, gone today,
Just the sort of customer for whom
Love is something to be thrown away
Eventually, like a broken comb.
Runing backwards as a palindrome,
Time will be deciphered anyway,
Though the implications of that poem
Originally resist a résumé.
Under the superstructure of the dome
The phone is dumb that had so much to say.

XIXe *Amérique, Combat*

Token of that humourous umpteenth
Memorable day misspent in bed,
A singular combat celebrated since
By incessant reruns in my head
At whose indecent vividness I wince,
All the evidence I loved you once
Recollected, everything you said
Elected as a god upon a plinth,
Take this text which you have never read
And never may, perhaps, erotic prints
Indelible as life itself whose length
Is measured in catastrophes instead
Of strophes, revised ineptly to the nth
Degree. Before you read me, we'll be dead.

XXe *Père Lachaise*

Death's exclusive suburb, where the doors
Open upon empty anterooms,
Welcomes a few tardy visitors
Cryptically on mortal afternoons.
The bogus nineteenth century adores,
Albeit in fantastic undertones,
What our sophisticated taste deplores,
Dramatic last words and attractive glooms.
Among marshals, musicians, courtesans and bores
Ranked according to profession, who presumes
To flout society's posthumous laws?
Statuettesque among the stolid tombs
Above our witty saint's dishonoured bones
Oscar's ithyphallic angel soars.

119

COMA BERENICES

Non omnia omina in anima.

Elusive as the features of a dream
One tries to piece together upon waking,
In my raised unconscious a familiar
Physical presence figures incognito,
One for whom I hankered all night long,
Victim of a strange metamorphosis:
Talented heels hardened into hooves,
Horns newly crescent among curls,
Rudimentary tail above fawn buttocks
Complete, with a canonical erection,
The change from innocent to satyr.

Not all signs are instinct in the mind,
Notably those cartoon constellations
Animated in consideration
To which we gave such funny names,
Weepy, Sleeping Beauty, and The Duck,
Splendid worlds in false perspective
Perverted by the point of view of time,
Receding from us at the speed of life
Nightly, unimportant in the morning,
Evanescent as delight.

I can feel my heart becoming dormant
Along with every other living thing,
Animals who find in hibernation
An alternative to suffering,
Trees that in their annual abandon
Seem to have forgotten about Spring.

Disguised beneath a mask of ashes,
The fire that laughed and chattered overnight
This morning mopes and grumbles.

Light and dark impartially divided,
Like white and black in an old-fashioned film,
In the guise of day and night dispute the world.
Today it looks as if the dark will win
Temporarily, until the solstice
When the light brigade begins again.

Faint spark, you were a part once of the darkness,
About to be absorbed into the sun,
Shining in inimitable witness,
A landmark of love's perihelion;
As my passion for you glows and crumbles,
A fading coal that used to be a flame,
A nightmare we can neither alter
Nor, even if we wanted to, relive,
Remoter every parsec, out of range
Before you disappear,
You leave me little to forgive
Beyond the familiar's becoming strange,
Everything that seemed quite near, or dear,
Reduced to the status of a souvenir.

That love of which you were the incarnation,
Which could not even really spell its name,
Idle, illiterate, and infantile,
Still in the sky of my imagination
Burns with an unmitigated flair,
Like a lock of Berenice's hair.

AFTERMATH

Ni Ange ni Bête

i

Psychology was Psyche's fault:
The bedside lamp, the burning drop
She let fall upon the flawless
Shoulder of the unconscious god.
For a moment though she saw him
Almost as he was, soft not hard
As she had always known him in the dark,
His nakedness no longer unashamed
But vulnerable as a mortal
Lost in a dream, the midnight black
Of his hair about the secret face
Of love: only for a moment
Before the immortal god
Woke and knew her and flew away.

ii

His departure an epiphany,
The work of night, without a word
Of apology he went away
As it was written, by another way
Into his own country. Boy or bird,
There for the time being he will stay.
In valediction what was she to say?
For all her insight Psyche cannot say
Candidly she understood his stay
Although offended by its brevity.
Was her anxiety absurd
In the light of yesterday?
Humiliated and bewildered
She will follow anyway.

iii

Above the unintelligible
Pack with human faces,
Wings like parentheses
Stuck upon his back,
He hovered out of reach,
Taunting and afraid,
Abruptly fallible,
Frantic to escape
The trap of consciousness.
What did his flight portend?
Faith might have divined.
Without an informing myth,
Bored beyond belief
Psyche can only guess.

iv

Compared to daily life her other tasks
Were child's play: sorting out the letters
Of the infatuated alphabet
To spell the name of her mistake;
Fetching refreshment from the dead;
The sort of tests that one is set in nightmare,
A bedtime story or an allegory,
Which must be solved before you wake,
Penitences possible except
Her final labour, to forget
The stolen sight of Love in bed
Beside her, naked and asleep,
The moving shadow on his cheek,
His surprised look before he fled.

COPIED IN CAMOES

Podeis-vos embarcar, que tendes vento
E mar tranquillo, para a pátria amada.
OS LUSIADAS, X, 143

Out of sight of land, with nothing to
Divert us but the instruments of reason,
Notoriously fallible and few,
And nothing obvious on the horizon,
The old world nearly vanished and the new
Not manifest as yet, our buoyant prison
Rations getting low, the water rotten,
The map of our discoveries forgotten;

Latitude and longitude the sole
Constituents in this liquid vacuum,
Having set out to explore the whole
Shebang, by the sea's triumphant tedium
Becalmed, our expedition its own goal,
Like someone in the middle of the night,
Sleepless, watching for the light
Of day it sometimes seems will never come;

As if the sun with one impatient stroke
Divided the unopened globe between us,
The known and the unknown, those old baroque
Antagonists of legend, Mars and Venus
Of whom I dreamt before I woke
Alone, adrift, my independent penis
Mast-rigid, riding the rambunctious waves—
It is the sense of home that soothes and saves—

The smell of land far out to sea
Overwhelms the sailor with surprised
Nostalgia for a catholic country
Whose shame-faced imperfections no one prized
Enough: familiarity
Is fatal, frequent favours are despised
Until—unless—they come to seem as subtle and
Exotic as the scent of sea on land.

SAMSON

Nihil alienum mihi humanum puto

At first I rather liked the Philistines
For their uninhibited style of living,
Domestic cooking and imported wines.
What if their morals were a little loose?
A fish-god can afford to be forgiving,
Unlike our xenophobic Lord of Hosts.

Nothing alien he considers human.
Nevertheless I made myself at home,
Thinking that we had enough in common
(Like the influential lanterns hung
From heaven's geodesic dome),
And started to forget my native tongue.

An expatriate, some would say, a traitor,
Ambitious only to end my days in peace,
Arrested as a foreign agitator,
Blind and bald, abandoned by my wife
To their theological police,
I was like one who has succumbed to life.

My exile brought me face to face with this
Decadent art décoratif;
Stifled by that ghastly edifice,
Ugly and intolerably smug,
(Man is a beast apart from his belief)
At last I brought the house down with a shrug.

A TROPHY

Alas: it is a devastated country
Through which a sullen enemy has passed,
With indifference laying waste
The passive landscape. Not one tree
It seems survives unscathed the sudden blast
Of infatuation, which has done its worst at last.
Where was Dislike, that dull sentry,
Once too often napping at her post
When destructive love forced entry?
Before it was declared the war was lost.

Time the pathetic arms were laid aside
That have proved so ineffectual,
Patience, courage, kindness, prudence, pride,
All obsolete before the secret, sexual
Weapons you had on your side,
Those wiles whereby intellectual
Defeat was deified,
As over all the ravaged countryside
Memory imposes far and wide
The desolation of the actual.

Of your triumph I am the sad trophy,
Whose conquests only pity can compile,
Whether won by excellence or guile.
Let the comforts of philosophy
Console the conquered for a while.
May your offenses with your defenses atrophy,
Your discontent be subject to your style,
And the ultimate catastrophe
Indicated by the creepy dial
Yield to your uncompromising smile.

MEMO TO GONGORA

To your language if not your native land,
Which is a tongue when all is said
That's done, perverse, gold, standard, and
Curiously conservative, as dead
As anything Amerigo invented,
I pilgrim with my accents in my hand
And your conceits unequalled in my head
Through volumes of rock and canticles of sand.
Like paradise, you are a promised land
Aflow with ilk and money, brine and wed-
lock, secrets that like circumstances stand
Unalterable, maps to be misread.
Were we translated here and now, instead
Of reading we might understand.